The
CLASSIC ITALIAN
COOKING COURSE

The CLASSIC ITALIAN COOKING COURSE

JENI WRIGHT AND ANGELA BOGGIANO

HERMES HOUSE

This edition first published in 1998 by Hermes House

HERMES HOUSE books are available for bulk purchase, for sales promotion and for
premium use. For details, write or call the sales director, Hermes House,
27 West 20th Street, New York, NY 10011; (800) 354-9657

Hermes House is an imprint of
Anness Publishing Inc

ISBN 1 84038 152 3

Publisher: Joanna Lorenz
Senior Editor: Linda Fraser
Designer: Siân Keogh
Jacket Designer: Lisa Tai
Photographer: William Lingwood
Home Economist: Lucy McKelvie, assisted by Sophie Wheeler
Stylist: Marian Price

Printed and bound in Singapore

1 3 5 7 9 10 8 6 4 2

Previously published as part of a larger compendium, *The Italian Ingredients Cookbook*.

NOTES
Large eggs should be used unless otherwise stated. (The recipe for Tiramisù contains
raw eggs and should be avoided by pregnant women, children and anyone who is unwell.)

Contents

Introduction

I talian cooking reflects the fact that the country was unified only in 1861. Until then, each region produced its own characteristic cuisine, relying exclusively on ingredients that could be gathered, cultivated or reared locally. Nowadays, of course, regional produce can be easily transported all over the country, but Italians still prefer to base their cooking on local ingredients, because they regard quality and freshness as more important than diversity and innovation. So the most flavorful sun–ripened tomatoes, eggplants and bell peppers are still found in the south, the freshest seafood is available along the coast, the finest hams come from the area where the pigs are raised, and so on. *La cucina italiana* remains distinctly regional; northern Italian cooking, for example, incorporates ingredients that are simply never found in the recipes of Sicily and Naples, and vice-versa. In the dairy-farming north, butter is used in place of the olive oil so prevalent in the south; bread and polenta are eaten instead of pasta. The only unifying feature is the insistence on high quality ingredients. Good food has always been essential to the Italian way of life. *La cucina italiana* is one of the oldest cooking cultures in the world, dating back to the Ancient Greeks and perhaps even earlier. The Romans adored food and

THIS ITALIAN BUTCHER'S SHOP (BELOW) NOT ONLY SELLS THE LOCAL *CINGHIALE* (WILD BOAR), BUT ALSO CURED MEATS, CHEESES AND OTHER ESSENTIAL COOKING INGREDIENTS.

often ate and drank to excess; it was they who really laid the foundations of Italian and European cuisine. The early Romans were peasant farmers who ate only the simple, rustic foods they could produce, such as grain, cheeses and olives. For them, meat was an unheard-of luxury; animals were bred to work in the fields and were too precious to eat. Trading links with other parts of the world, however, encouraged Roman farmers to cultivate new vegetables and fruits and, of course, grapes, while their trade in salt and exotic spices enabled them to preserve and pickle all kinds of meat, game and fish. Food became a near-obsession and ever more elaborate dishes were devised to be served at the decadent and orgiastic banquets for which the Romans were famed. The decline and fall of the Roman Empire led inevitably to a deterioration in the quality of cooking and a return to simple, basic foods. For centuries, regional cuisine reverted to its original uncomplicated style. With the Renaissance, however, came great wealth and a new interest in elaborate food. Once again, rich families strove to outdo each other with lavish banquets where courses of rich, extravagant foods were served—truffles, song–birds, game, desserts dripping with honey and spices—all washed down with vast quantities of wine. The poor, of course, continued to subsist on the simple foods they

OLIVES (TOP) GROWING IN GROVES ALONGSIDE GRAPE VINES ON AN UMBRIAN HILLSIDE, AND A SELECTION OF CURED SAUSAGES AND AIR-DRIED PROSCIUTTO (ABOVE) ARE JUST TWO OF THE VAST ARRAY OF TRADITIONAL ITALIAN INGREDIENTS THAT ARE NOW EXPORTED AROUND THE WORLD.

ITALIAN COOKS INSIST ON HIGH-QUALITY COOKING INGREDIENTS, AND EVEN LOCAL DELICATESSENS (RIGHT) ARE PACKED FULL OF FRESH AND PRESERVED INGREDIENTS AND OTHER FOODS—FRUITY CAKES AND CRISP COOKIES, SUCH AS *PANFORTE* AND *CANTUCCI*, DRIED *FAGIOLI* (BEANS), FLAVORFUL OLIVE OILS AND VINEGARS, *PROSCIUTTO CRUDO* (CURED HAMS), TRADITIONAL CHEESES, SUCH AS PARMIGIANO REGGIANO, PICKLES AND PRESERVES, MARINATED OLIVES, CANNED TOMATOES AND BOTTLED SAUCES.

THE SUN-DRENCHED SOUTHERN REGIONS OF ITALY PROVIDE ESSENTIAL PANTRY INGREDIENTS, SUCH AS FULL-FLAVORED GREEN AND BLACK OLIVES AND DELICIOUS SUN-DRIED TOMATOES.

had always eaten, but the wealthier middle classes developed a taste for fine foods and created their own bourgeois dishes. The finer features of Italian cooking even reached the French, when Catherine de' Medici went to Paris to marry the future Henri II, taking fifty of her own cooks with her. They introduced new ingredients and cooking techniques to France and in return learned the art of French cuisine. In those regions of Italy that border France, you can still find reciprocal influences of French classical cooking but, generally speaking, Italians do not like elaborately sauced dishes, preferring to let the natural flavors of their raw ingredients speak for themselves.

The essence of Italian cooking today is simplicity. The Italian way of cooking fish is a good example of this. In coastal areas, freshly caught fish is most often simply grilled over hot coals, then served with nothing more than a splash of extra virgin olive oil, a wedge of lemon and freshly ground black pepper. Recipes such as *carpaccio di tonno*, in which the fish is so delicious raw that cooking seems unnecessary, and *branzino al forno*, where the delicate flavor of fennel is used to complement rather than obscure the fresh taste of the fish, are typically simple, as is *grigliata di calamari*, squid grilled with chilies to reflect its robust character.

Italians learn to appreciate good food when they are young children, and eating is one of the major pleasures of the day, no matter what the day of the week or time of the year. Witness an Italian family gathered around the Sunday lunch table in a local restaurant, and consider how the Italian menu of *antipasto* followed by pasta, rice or gnocchi, then fish, meat and vegetables served in sequence is devised so that each can be savored separately—both the food and the occasion are to be enjoyed as long as possible. The first course, or *antipasto*, is a unique feature. In restaurants, this can be a vast array of different dishes, both hot and cold, from which diners can choose as few or as many as they wish. At home with the family, it is more likely to be a slice or two of *salame* or *prosciutto crudo* with fresh figs or melon, if these are in season. But no matter how humble or grand the setting or the occasion, the *antipasto* is always visually tempting. Colorful dishes such as *calamari in insalata alla genovese* and *peperoni arrostiti con pesto*, are typical in this way.

The variety and diversity of the Italian ingredients available at supermarkets and delicatessens will surely inspire you to concoct any number of delicious meals, from a simple dish of pasta to a full-blown four-course dinner. A plate of *antipasto* followed by pasta or risotto flavored with seasonal ingredients, then simply-cooked meat or fish and finally a local cheese and fruit makes a veritable feast. You could prepare a different meal along these lines every day of the year and almost never repeat the same combination. If you visit Italy, avail yourself of the wonderful local ingredients to prepare a menu full of the flavors of the region. Every area has its own special delights that make cooking a real pleasure.

FRESH INGREDIENTS ARE HIGHLY PRIZED BY ITALIAN COOKS AND ARE OFTEN SOLD AT THE LOCAL OUTDOOR MARKETS: DOZENS OF *CARCIOFI* (ARTICHOKES) ARE TIED READY FOR TRANSPORT TO A LOCAL MARKET (BELOW), AND AN OUTDOOR STALL IS PILED HIGH WITH A TYPICALLY WIDE SELECTION OF HIGH-QUALITY FRESH HERBS AND SALAD GREENS, VEGETABLES AND FRUITS (BOTTOM).

Antipasti

Antipasto means "before the meal," and no
respectable Italian meal would start without it.
The recipes in this chapter are typical of Italian
antipasti—appetizing and easy on the eye, light and
tasty. Vegetables, fish and salads are the mainstay,
not only for their lightness and freshness,
but also for their color.

Roast Bell Pepper Terrine

Torta di peperoni al forno

This terrine is perfect for a dinner party because it tastes better if made ahead. Prepare the salsa on the day of serving. Serve with hot Italian bread.

Ingredients

8 bell peppers (red, yellow and orange)
3 cups mascarpone cheese
3 eggs, separated
2 tbsp each roughly chopped flat-leaf
    parsley and shredded basil
2 large garlic cloves, roughly chopped
2 red, yellow or orange bell peppers,
    seeded and roughly chopped
2 tbsp extra virgin olive oil
2 tsp balsamic vinegar
a few basil sprigs
pinch of sugar
salt and freshly ground black pepper
serves 8

1 Place the peppers under a hot broiler for 8–10 minutes, turning them frequently until the skins are charred and blistered on all sides. Put the hot peppers in ziplock bags, seal and set aside until cold.

2 ▲ Rub off the pepper skins under cold running water. Break open the flesh and rub out the cores and seeds. Drain the peppers, dry them on paper towels, then cut seven of them lengthwise into thin, even-size strips. Reserve the remaining pepper for the salsa.

Variation

For a low-fat version of this terrine, use ricotta cheese instead of the mascarpone.

3 Put the mascarpone cheese in a bowl with the egg yolks, herbs and half the garlic. Add salt and pepper to taste. Beat well. In a separate bowl, whisk the egg whites to a soft peak, then fold into the cheese mixture until evenly incorporated.

4 ▲ Preheat the oven to 350°F. Line the base of a lightly oiled 2-pound loaf pan. Put one-third of the cheese mixture in the pan and spread level. Arrange half the pepper strips on top in an even layer. Repeat until all the cheese and peppers are used.

5 Cover the pan with foil and place in a roasting pan. Pour in boiling water to come halfway up the sides of the pan. Bake for 1 hour. Let cool in the water bath, then lift out and chill overnight.

6 A few hours before serving, make the salsa. Place the remaining roast pepper and fresh peppers in a food processor. Add the remaining garlic, oil and vinegar. Set aside a few basil leaves for garnishing and add the rest to the processor. Process until finely chopped. Transfer the mixture to a bowl, add sugar and salt and pepper to taste and mix well. Cover and chill until ready to serve.

7 Turn out the terrine, peel off the paper and slice thickly. Garnish with the basil leaves and serve cold, with the sweet pepper salsa.

Pan-fried Chicken Liver Salad

Insalata di fegatini

This Florentine salad uses vin santo, a sweet dessert wine from Tuscany, but this is not

essential—any dessert wine will do, or a sweet or cream sherry.

Ingredients

3 oz fresh baby spinach leaves
3 oz lollo rosso or red leaf lettuce
5 tbsp olive oil
1 tbsp butter
8 oz chicken livers, trimmed and thinly
    sliced
3 tbsp vin santo
2–3 oz fresh Parmesan cheese, shaved
    into curls
salt and freshly ground black pepper

serves 4

1 ▲ Wash and dry the spinach and lollo rosso. Tear the leaves into a large bowl, season with salt and pepper to taste and toss gently to mix.

2 ▲ Heat 2 tablespoons of the oil with the butter in a large heavy frying pan. When foaming, add the chicken livers and toss over medium to high heat for 5 minutes or until the livers are browned on the outside but still pink in the center. Remove from the heat.

3 ▲ Remove the livers from the pan with a slotted spoon, drain them on paper towels, then place on top of the spinach.

4 ▲ Return the pan to medium heat, add the remaining oil and the vin santo and stir until sizzling.

5 Pour the hot dressing over the spinach and livers and toss to coat. Put the salad in a serving bowl and sprinkle the Parmesan shavings on top. Serve immediately.

Genoese Squid Salad

Calamari in insalata alla genovese

This is a good salad for summer, when green beans and new potatoes are at their best.

Serve it for a first course or light lunch.

Ingredients

1 lb prepared squid, cut into rings
4 garlic cloves, roughly chopped
1¼ cups Italian red wine
1 lb waxy new potatoes,
    scrubbed clean
8 oz green beans, trimmed and cut into
    short lengths
2–3 drained sun-dried tomatoes in oil,
    thinly sliced lengthwise
4 tbsp extra virgin olive oil
1 tbsp red wine vinegar
salt and freshly ground black pepper

serves 4–6

Cook's Tip

The French potato called Charlotte is perfect for this type of salad because it retains its shape and does not break up when boiled. Prepared squid can be bought at supermarkets with fresh fish counters, and at fishmongers.

1 ▲ Preheat the oven to 350°F. Put the squid rings in an earthenware dish with half the garlic, the wine and pepper to taste. Cover and cook for 45 minutes or until the squid is tender.

2 Put the potatoes in a saucepan, cover with cold water and add a good pinch of salt. Bring to a boil, cover and simmer for 15–20 minutes or until tender. Using a slotted spoon, lift out the potatoes and set aside. Add the beans to the boiling water and cook for 3 minutes. Drain.

3 ▲ When the potatoes are cool enough to handle, slice them thickly on the diagonal and place them in a bowl with the warm beans and sun-dried tomatoes. Whisk the oil, wine vinegar and the remaining garlic in a pitcher and add salt and pepper to taste. Pour over the potato mixture.

4 Drain the squid and discard the wine and garlic. Add the squid to the potato mixture and fold very gently to mix. Arrange the salad on individual plates and grind pepper liberally all over. Serve warm.

Tuna Carpaccio

Carpaccio di tonno

Fillet of beef is most often used for carpaccio, but meaty fish such as tuna—and swordfish —make an unusual change. The secret is to slice the fish wafer thin, made possible by freezing the fish first, a technique used by the Japanese for making sashimi.

Ingredients

2 fresh tuna steaks, about 1 pound total
  weight
4 tbsp extra virgin olive oil
1 tbsp balsamic vinegar
1 tsp superfine sugar
2 tbsp drained bottled green peppercorns
  or capers
salt and freshly ground black pepper
lemon wedges and green salad,
  · to serve
serves 4

Cook's Tip

Raw fish is safe to eat as long as it is very fresh, so check with your fishmonger before purchase, and make and serve carpaccio on the same day. Do not buy fish that has been frozen and thawed.

1 ▲ Remove the skin from each tuna steak and place each steak between two sheets of plastic wrap or waxed paper. Pound with a rolling pin until flattened slightly.

2 Roll up the tuna as tightly as possible, then wrap tightly in plastic wrap and place in the freezer for 4 hours or until firm.

3 ▲ Unwrap the tuna and cut vertically into the thinnest possible slices. Arrange on individual plates.

4 Whisk together the remaining ingredients, season and pour over the tuna. Cover and let come to room temperature for 30 minutes before serving with lemon wedges and green salad.

Marinated Vegetable Antipasto   *Verdura marinata per antipasto*

Antipasto means "before the meal" and traditionally consists of a selection of marinated vegetable dishes served with good Italian salami and thin slices of prosciutto. Serve in attractive bowls, with plenty of fresh crusty bread.

Ingredients

For the peppers
3 red bell peppers
3 yellow bell peppers
4 garlic cloves, sliced
handful fresh basil, plus extra to garnish
extra virgin olive oil
salt and freshly ground black pepper

For the mushrooms
1 lb open cap mushrooms
4 tbsp extra virgin olive oil
1 large garlic clove, crushed
1 tbsp chopped fresh rosemary
1 cup dry white wine
fresh rosemary sprigs, to garnish

For the olives
1 dried red chili, crushed
grated rind of 1 lemon
$\frac{1}{2}$ cup extra virgin olive oil
1$\frac{1}{3}$ cups Italian black olives
2 tbsp chopped fresh flat-leaf parsley
1 lemon wedge, to serve

serves 4

1 ▲ Place the peppers under a hot broiler. Turn occasionally until they are blackened and blistered all over. Remove from the heat and place in a large plastic bag. When cool, remove the skin, halve the peppers and remove the seeds. Cut the flesh into strips lengthwise and place them in a bowl with the sliced garlic and basil leaves. Add salt, to taste, cover with oil and marinate for 3–4 hours before serving, tossing occasionally. When serving, garnish with more basil leaves.

2 Thickly slice the mushrooms and place in a large bowl. Heat the oil in a small pan and add the garlic and rosemary. Pour in the wine. Bring the mixture to a boil, then lower the heat and simmer for 3 minutes. Add salt and pepper to taste.

3 ▲ Pour the mixture over the mushrooms. Mix well and let cool, stirring occasionally. Cover and marinate overnight. Serve at room temperature, garnished with rosemary sprigs.

4 ▲ Prepare the olives. Place the chili and lemon rind in a small pan with the oil. Heat gently for about 3 minutes. Add the olives and heat for 1 more minute. Pour into a bowl and let cool. Marinate overnight. Sprinkle on the parsley just before serving with the lemon wedge.

Cook's Tip
The pepper antipasto can be stored in the refrigerator for up to 2 weeks covered in olive oil in an airtight jar.

Stuffed Roast Peppers with Pesto

Peperoni arrostiti con pesto

Serve these scallop- and pesto-filled red bell peppers with Italian bread, such as ciabatta or focaccia, to mop up the garlicky juices.

Ingredients
4 squat red bell peppers
2 large garlic cloves, cut into thin slivers
4 tbsp olive oil
4 shelled scallops
3 tbsp pesto
salt and freshly ground black pepper
freshly grated Parmesan cheese,
   to serve
salad leaves and fresh basil sprigs,
   to garnish
serves 4

Cook's Tip
Scallops are available at most fishmongers and supermarkets with fresh fish counters. Never cook scallops for longer than the time stated in the recipe or they will be tough and rubbery.

1 Preheat the oven to 350°F. Cut the peppers in half lengthwise, through their stalks. Scrape out and discard the cores and seeds. Wash the pepper shells and pat dry.

2 ▲ Put the peppers, cut-side up, in an oiled roasting pan. Divide the slivers of garlic equally among them and sprinkle with salt and pepper to taste. Spoon the oil into the peppers, then roast for 40 minutes.

3 ▲ Cut each of the shelled scallops in half to make two flat discs. Remove the peppers from the oven and place a scallop half in each pepper half. Top with pesto.

4 Return the pan to the oven and roast for 10 more minutes. Transfer the peppers to individual serving plates, sprinkle with grated Parmesan and garnish each plate with a few salad leaves and fresh basil sprigs. Serve warm.

Mozzarella Skewers

Spiedini alla romana

Stacks of flavor—layers of oven-baked mozzarella, tomatoes, basil and bread.

Ingredients

12 slices white country bread, each
    about ½-in thick
3 tbsp olive oil
8 oz mozzarella cheese, cut into
    ¼-in slices
3 plum tomatoes, cut into
    ¼-in slices
½ cup fresh basil leaves, plus extra to
    garnish
salt and freshly ground black pepper
2 tbsp chopped fresh flat-
    leaf parsley, to garnish
serves 4

Cook's Tip

If you use wooden skewers, soak
them in water first, to prevent
scorching.

1 ▲ Preheat the oven to 425°F. Trim
the crusts from the bread and cut
each slice into four equal squares.
Arrange on a baking sheet and brush
on one side (or both sides) with half
the olive oil. Bake for 3–5 minutes,
until the squares are pale gold.

2 Remove from the oven and place
the bread squares on a board with
the other ingredients.

3 ▲ Make 16 stacks, each starting
with a square of bread, then a slice of
mozzarella topped with a slice of
tomato and a basil leaf. Sprinkle with
salt and pepper, then repeat, ending
with the bread. Push a skewer
through each stack and place on
the baking sheet. Drizzle with the
remaining oil and bake for
10–15 minutes, until the cheese
begins to melt. Garnish with fresh
basil leaves and serve scattered with
chopped fresh flat leaf parsley.

Eggplant Fritters

Frittelle di melanzane

These simply delicious fritters make a superb appetizer or vegetarian supper dish.

Ingredients

1 large eggplant, about 1½ lb, cut into
    ½-in thick slices
2 tbsp olive oil
1 egg, lightly beaten
2 garlic cloves, crushed
4 tbsp chopped fresh parsley
2¼ cups fresh white bread crumbs
generous 1 cup grated
    Parmesan cheese
generous 1 cup feta cheese, crumbled
3 tbsp flour
sunflower oil, for shallow frying
salt and freshly ground black pepper

To serve

plain yogurt, flavored with fried red
    chilies and cumin seeds
lime wedges
serves 4

1 ▲ Preheat the oven to 375°F.
Brush the eggplant slices with the
olive oil, then place them on a
baking sheet and bake for about
20 minutes until golden and tender.
Chop the slices finely and place them
in a bowl with the egg, garlic, parsley,
bread crumbs, Parmesan and feta.
Add salt and pepper to taste, and mix
well. Let the mixture rest for about
20 minutes. If the mixture looks very
sloppy, add more bread crumbs.

2 ▲ Divide the mixture into eight
balls and flatten them slightly. Place
the flour on a plate and season with
salt and pepper. Coat the fritters in
the flour, shaking off any excess.

3 Shallow fry the fritters in batches
for 1 minute on each side, until
golden brown. Drain on paper
towels and serve with the flavored
yogurt and lime wedges.

Soups

· ·

The Italians are avid soup eaters, and some of the best soups in the world come from Italy. Clear broth, brodo, *and delicate puréed soups are served as a first course before a main meal. More substantial chunky soups,* minestre, *are often main meals in themselves, usually served in the evening if the main meal of the day has been at lunchtime.*

Wild Mushroom Soup

Zuppa di porcini

Wild mushrooms are expensive. Dried porcini have an intense flavor, so only a small quantity is needed. The beef stock may seem unusual in a vegetable soup, but it helps to strengthen the earthy flavor of the mushrooms.

Ingredients

2 cups dried porcini mushrooms
2 tbsp olive oil
1 tbsp butter
2 leeks, thinly sliced
2 shallots, roughly chopped
1 garlic clove, roughly chopped
3 cups fresh wild mushrooms
5 cups beef stock
$\frac{1}{2}$ tsp dried thyme
$\frac{2}{3}$ cup heavy cream
salt and freshly ground black pepper
fresh thyme sprigs, to garnish
serves 4

Cook's Tip

Porcini are cepes. Italian cooks would make this soup with a combination of fresh and dried cepes, but if fresh cepes are difficult to obtain, you can use other wild mushrooms, such as chanterelles.

1 ▲ Put the dried porcini in a bowl, add 1 cup warm water and let soak for 20–30 minutes. Lift them out of the liquid and squeeze over the bowl to remove as much of the soaking liquid as possible. Strain all the liquid and reserve to use later. Finely chop the porcini.

2 Heat the oil and butter in a large saucepan until foaming. Add the sliced leeks, chopped shallots and garlic and cook gently for about 5 minutes, stirring frequently, until softened but not colored.

3 ▲ Chop or slice the fresh mushrooms and add to the pan. Stir over medium heat for a few minutes until they begin to soften. Pour in the stock and bring to a boil. Add the porcini, soaking liquid, dried thyme and salt and pepper. Lower the heat, half cover the pan and simmer gently for 30 minutes, stirring occasionally.

4 ▲ Pour about three-quarters of the soup into a blender or food processor and process until smooth. Return to the soup remaining in the pan, stir in the cream and heat through. Check the consistency and add more stock if the soup is too thick. Taste for seasoning. Serve hot, garnished with thyme sprigs.

Tomato and Fresh Basil Soup   *Crema di pomodori al basilico*

A soup for late summer when fresh tomatoes are at their most flavorful.

Ingredients

1 tbsp olive oil
2 tbsp butter
1 medium onion, finely chopped
2 pounds ripe Italian plum tomatoes,
    roughly chopped
1 garlic clove, roughly chopped
about 3 cups chicken or vegetable stock
$\frac{1}{2}$ cup dry white wine
2 tbsp sun-dried tomato paste
2 tbsp shredded fresh basil, plus a few
    whole leaves, to garnish
$\frac{2}{3}$ cup heavy cream
salt and freshly ground black pepper

serves 4–6

1 ▲ Heat the oil and butter in a large saucepan until foaming. Add the onion and cook gently for about 5 minutes, stirring frequently, until softened but not brown.

2 ▲ Stir in the chopped tomatoes and garlic, then add the stock, white wine and sun-dried tomato paste, with salt and pepper to taste. Bring to a boil, then lower the heat, half cover the pan and simmer gently for 20 minutes, stirring occasionally to prevent the tomatoes from sticking to the base of the pan.

3 ▲ Process the soup with the shredded basil in a blender or food processor, then press through a sieve into a clean pan.

4 ▲ Add the heavy cream and heat through, stirring. Do not let the soup approach the boiling point. Check the consistency and add more stock if necessary and then taste for seasoning. Pour into heated bowls and garnish with basil. Serve immediately.

Variation

The soup can also be served chilled. Pour it into a container after straining and chill for at least 4 hours. Serve in chilled bowls.

Minestrone with Pasta and Beans

Minestrone alla milanese

This classic minestrone from Lombardy includes pancetta for a pleasant touch of saltiness.

Milanese cooks vary the recipe according to what is at hand, and you can do the same.

Ingredients

3 tbsp olive oil
4 oz pancetta, any rinds removed,
　roughly chopped
2–3 celery stalks, finely chopped
3 medium carrots, finely chopped
1 medium onion, finely chopped
1–2 garlic cloves, crushed
2 cans (14 oz each) chopped tomatoes
about 4 cups chicken stock
1 can (14 oz) cannellini beans, drained
　and rinsed
1/2 cup macaroni
2–4 tbsp chopped flat-leaf parsley,
　to taste
salt and freshly ground black pepper
shaved Parmesan cheese, to serve
serves 4

Variation

Use long-grain rice instead of the pasta, and borlotti beans instead of cannellini.

1 ▲ Heat the oil in a large saucepan. Add the pancetta, celery, carrots and onion and cook over low heat for 5 minutes, stirring constantly, until the vegetables are softened.

2 Add the garlic and tomatoes, breaking them up well with a wooden spoon. Pour in the stock. Add salt and pepper to taste and bring to a boil. Half cover the pan, lower the heat and simmer gently for about 20 minutes, until the vegetables are soft.

3 ▲ Drain the beans and add them to the pan with the macaroni. Bring to a boil again. Cover, lower the heat and continue to simmer for about 20 more minutes. Check the consistency and add more stock if necessary. Stir in the parsley and taste for seasoning.

4 Serve hot, sprinkled with plenty of Parmesan cheese. This makes a meal in itself if served with chunks of crusty Italian bread.

Summer Minestrone

Minestrone estivo

This brightly colored, fresh-tasting soup makes the most of summer vegetables.

Ingredients

3 tbsp olive oil
1 large onion, finely chopped
1 tbsp sun-dried tomato paste
1 lb ripe Italian plum tomatoes, peeled
　and finely chopped
8 oz green zucchini, trimmed and roughly
　chopped
8 oz yellow summer squash, trimmed and
　roughly chopped
3 waxy new potatoes, diced
2 garlic cloves, crushed
about 5 cups chicken stock or water
1/4 cup shredded fresh basil
2/3 cup grated Parmesan cheese
salt and freshly ground black pepper
serves 4

1 ▲ Heat the oil in a large saucepan, add the onion and cook gently for about 5 minutes, stirring constantly, until softened. Stir in the sun-dried tomato paste, chopped tomatoes, zucchini, squash, diced potatoes and garlic. Mix well and cook gently for 10 minutes, uncovered, shaking the pan frequently to prevent the vegetables from sticking to the base.

2 ▲ Pour in the stock. Bring to a boil, lower the heat, half cover the pan and simmer gently for 15 minutes or until the vegetables are just tender. Add more stock if necessary.

3 Remove the pan from the heat and stir in the basil and half the cheese. Taste for seasoning. Serve hot, sprinkled with the remaining cheese.

Clam and Pasta Soup

Zuppa alle vongole

This soup is a play on a popular pasta dish—spaghetti alle vongole—using pantry

ingredients. Serve it with hot focaccia or ciabatta for an informal supper with friends.

Ingredients

2 tbsp olive oil
1 large onion, finely chopped
2 garlic cloves, crushed
1 can (14 oz) chopped tomatoes
1 tbsp sun-dried tomato paste
1 tsp sugar
1 tsp dried mixed herbs
about 3 cups fish or vegetable stock
2/3 cup red wine
1/2 cup small pasta shapes
1 jar or can (5 oz) clams in
    natural juice
2 tbsp finely chopped flat-leaf parsley,
    plus a few whole leaves,
    to garnish
salt and freshly ground black pepper

serves 4

1 ▲ Heat the oil in a large saucepan. Cook the onion gently for 5 minutes, stirring frequently, until softened.

2 ▲ Add the garlic, tomatoes, tomato paste, sugar, herbs, stock and wine, with salt and pepper to taste. Bring to a boil. Lower the heat, half cover the pan and simmer for 10 minutes, stirring occasionally.

3 ▲ Add the pasta and continue simmering, uncovered, for about 10 minutes or until *al dente*. Stir occasionally, to prevent the pasta shapes from sticking together.

Cook's Tip

This soup has a fuller flavor if it is made the day before and reheated.

4 ▲ Add the clams and their juice to the soup and heat through for 3–4 minutes, adding more stock if required. Do not let it boil or the clams will be tough. Remove from the heat, stir in the parsley and taste the soup for seasoning. Serve hot, sprinkled with coarsely ground black pepper and parsley leaves.

Tuscan Bean Soup
Zuppa di fagioli alla toscana

There are lots of versions of this wonderful soup. This one uses cannellini beans, leeks, cabbage and good olive oil—and tastes even better reheated.

Ingredients

3 tbsp extra virgin olive oil
1 onion, roughly chopped
2 leeks, roughly chopped
1 large potato, peeled and diced
2 garlic cloves, finely chopped
5 cups vegetable stock
1 can (14 oz) cannellini beans, drained,
    liquid reserved
1/2 (6 oz) Savoy cabbage, shredded
3 tbsp chopped fresh flat-
    leaf parsley
2 tbsp chopped fresh oregano
1 cup Parmesan cheese, shaved
salt and freshly ground black pepper

For the garlic toasts

2–3 tbsp extra virgin olive oil
6 thick slices country bread
1 garlic clove, peeled and bruised

serves 4

3 ▲ Stir in the cabbage and beans, with half the herbs, season and cook for 10 more minutes. Spoon about one-third of the soup into a food processor or blender and process until fairly smooth. Return to the soup in the pan, taste for seasoning and heat through for 5 minutes.

4 ▲ Meanwhile, make the garlic toasts. Drizzle a little oil over the slices of bread, then rub both sides of each slice with the garlic. Toast until browned on both sides. Ladle the soup into bowls. Sprinkle with the remaining herbs and the Parmesan shavings. Add a drizzle of olive oil and serve with the toasts.

1 ▲ Heat the oil in a large saucepan and gently cook the onion, leeks, potato and garlic for 4–5 minutes.

2 ▲ Pour in the stock and liquid from the beans. Cover and simmer for 15 minutes.

Pasta & Gnocchi

····················

In Italy, pasta and gnocchi are traditionally served as a first course after the antipasto and before the second course of fish or meat. Everyday dishes are often simple, served with nothing more than olive oil or butter, grated Parmesan and basil. Outside of Italy there are no hard-and-fast rules, and nowadays people eat pasta and gnocchi whenever they like.

How to Make Egg Pasta by Hand

This classic recipe for egg noodles from Emilia-Romagna calls for just three ingredients: flour and eggs, with a little salt. In other regions of Italy water, milk or oil are sometimes added. Use plain unbleached white flour, and large eggs. As a general guide, use ½ cup of flour to each egg Quantities will vary with the exact size of the eggs.

To serve 3—4
2 eggs, salt
1 cup flour

To serve 4—6
3 eggs, salt
1½ cups flour

To serve 6—8
4 eggs, salt
2 cups flour

1 ▲ Place the flour in the center of a clean smooth work surface. Make a well in the middle. Break the eggs into the well. Add a pinch of salt.

2 Start beating the eggs with a fork, gradually drawing the flour from the inside walls of the well. As the paste thickens, continue the mixing with your hands. Incorporate as much flour as possible until the mixture forms a mass. It will still be lumpy. If it still sticks to your hands, add a little more flour. Set the dough aside. Scrape off all traces of the dough from the work surface until it is perfectly smooth. Wash and dry your hands.

About Pasta

Most pasta is made from durum wheat flour and water – durum is a special kind of wheat with a very high protein content. Egg pasta, *pasta all'uova*, contains flour and eggs, and is used for flat noodles such as tagliatelle, or for lasagne. Very little whole wheat pasta is eaten in Italy, but it is quite popular in other countries.

All these types of pasta are available dried in packets, and will keep almost indefinitely. Fresh pasta is now more widely available and can be bought in most supermarkets. It can be very good, but can never compare to home-made egg pasta.

Pasta comes in countless shapes and sizes. It is very difficult to give a definite list, as the names for the shapes vary from country to country. In some cases, just within Italy, the same shape can appear with several different names, depending upon which region it is in. The pasta shapes called for in this book, as well as many others, are illustrated in the introduction. The most common names have been listed.

Most of the recipes in this book specify the pasta shape most appropriate for a particular sauce. They can, of course, be replaced with another kind. A general rule is that long pasta goes better with tomato or thinner sauces, while short pasta is best for chunkier, meatier sauces. But this rule should not be followed too rigidly. Part of the fun of cooking and eating pasta is in the endless combinations of sauce and pasta shapes.

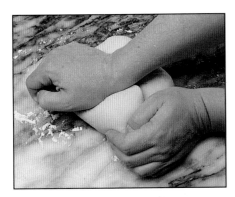

3 ▲ Lightly flour the work surface. Knead the dough by pressing it away from you with the heel of your hands, and then folding it over towards you. Repeat this action over and over, turning the dough as you knead. Work for about 10 minutes, or until the dough is smooth and elastic.

4 ▲ If you are using more than 2 eggs, divide the dough in half. Flour the rolling pin and the work surface. Pat the dough into a disc and begin rolling it out into a flat circle, rotating it one quarter turn after each roll to keep its shape round. Roll until the disc is about ⅛ in thick.

5 ▲ Roll out the dough until it is paper-thin by rolling up onto the

rolling pin and simultaneously giving a sideways stretching with the hands. Wrap the near edge of the dough around the center of the rolling pin, and begin rolling the dough up away from you. As you roll back and forth, slide your hands from the center towards the outer edges of the pin, stretching and thinning out the pasta.

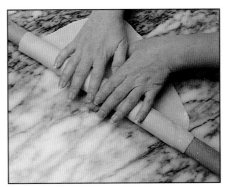

6 ▲ Quickly repeat these movements until about two-thirds of the sheet of pasta is wrapped around the pin. Lift and turn the wrapped pasta sheet about 45° before unrolling it. Repeat the rolling and stretching process, starting from a new point of the sheet each time to keep it evenly thin. By the end (this process should not last more than 8 to 10 minutes or the dough will lose its elasticity) the whole sheet should be smooth and almost transparent. If the dough is still sticky, lightly flour your hands as you continue rolling and stretching.

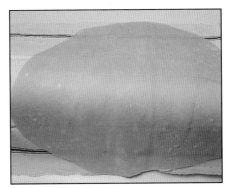

7 ▲ If you are making noodles (tagliatelle, fettuccine etc.) lay a clean dish towel on a table or other flat surface, and unroll the pasta sheet on it, letting about a third of the sheet hang over the edge of the table. Rotate

the dough every 10 minutes. Roll out the second sheet of dough if you are using more than 2 eggs. After 25–30 minutes the pasta will have dried enough to cut. Do not overdry or the pasta will crack as it is cut.

8 ▲ To cut tagliatelle, fettuccine or tagliolini, fold the sheet of pasta into a flat roll about 4 in wide. Cut across the roll to form noodles of the desired width. Tagliolini is ⅛ in; Fettuccine is ⅙ in; Tagliatelle is ¼ in. After cutting, open out the noodles, and let them dry for about 5 minutes before cooking. These noodles may be stored for some weeks without refrigeration. Allow them to dry completely before storing them, uncovered, in a dry cupboard.

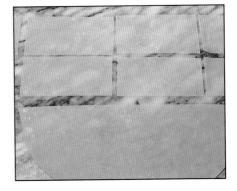

9 ▲ To cut the pasta for lasagne or pappardelle, do not fold or dry the rolled out dough. Lasagne is made by cutting rectangles approximately 5 in by 3½ in. Pappardelle are large noodles cut with a fluted pastry wheel. They are about ¾ in wide.

Egg Pasta Made by Machine

Making pasta with a machine is quick and easy. The results are perhaps not quite as fine as with handmade pasta, but they are certainly better than store-bought pastas.

You will need a pasta-making machine, either hand-cranked or electric. Use the same proportions of eggs, flours and salt as for Handmade Egg Pasta.

1 ▲ Place the flour in the center of a clean smooth work surface. Make a well in the middle. Break the eggs into the well. Add a pinch of salt. Start beating the eggs with a fork, gradually drawing the flour from the inside walls of the well. As the paste thickens, continue mixing with your hands. Incorporate as much flour as possible until the mixture forms a mass. It will still be lumpy. If it sticks to your hands, add a little more flour. Set the dough aside and scrape the work surface clean.

2 ▲ Set the machine rollers at their widest (kneading) setting. Pull off a piece of dough the size of a small

orange. Place the remaining dough between two soup plates. Feed the dough through the rollers. Fold it in half, end to end, and feed it through again 7 or 8 times, turning it and folding it over after each kneading. The dough should be smooth and fairly evenly rectangular. If it sticks to the machine, brush with flour. Lay it out on a lightly floured work surface or on a clean dish towel, and repeat with the remaining dough, broken into pieces the same size.

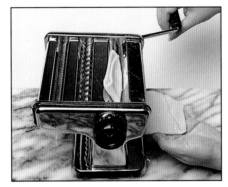

3 ▲ Adjust the machine to the next line setting. Feed each strip through once only, and replace on the drying surface. Keep them in the order in which they were first kneaded.

4 ▲ Reset the machine to the next setting. Repeat, passing each strip through once. Repeat for each remaining roller setting until the pasta is the right thickness — for most purposes this is given by the next to last setting, except for very delicate strips such as tagliolini, or for ravioli. If the pasta strips get too long, cut them in half to facilitate handling.

5 ▲ When all the strips are the desired thickness they may be machine-cut into noodles, or hand-cut for lasagne or pappardelle, as described for handmade pasta earlier. When making noodles, be sure the pasta is fairly dry, but not brittle, or the noodles may stick togther when cut. Select the desired width of cutter, and feed the strips through.

6 Separate the noodles, and leave to dry for at least 15 minutes before using. They may be stored for some weeks without refrigeration. Allow them to dry completely before storing them, uncovered, in a dry cupboard. They may also be frozen, first loose on trays and then packed together.

7 If you are making stuffed pasta (ravioli, cannelloni etc.) do not let the pasta strips dry out before filling them, but proceed immediately with the individual recipes.

How to Cook Dried Pasta

Store-bought and home-made pasta are cooked in the same way, though the timings vary greatly. Home-made pasta cooks virtually in the time it takes for the water to return to a boil after it is put in.

1 Always cook pasta in a large pot with a generous amount of rapidly boiling water. Use at least 5 cups of water to each ½ cup pasta.

2 ▲ The water should be salted at least 2 minutes before the pasta is added, to give the salt time to dissolve. Add about 1½ tbsp salt per 2 cups of pasta. You may want to vary the saltiness of the cooking water.

3 ▲ Drop the pasta into the boiling water all at once. Use a wooden spoon to help ease long pasta in as it softens, to prevent it from breaking. Stir frequently to prevent the pasta sticking to itself or to the pan. Cook the pasta at a fast boil, but be prepared to lower the heat if it boils over.

4 Timing is critical in pasta cooking. Follow package indications for store-bought pasta, but it is best in all cases to test for doneness by tasting, several times if necessary. In Italy pasta is always eaten *al dente*, which mens firm to the bite. Cooked this way it is just tender, but its "soul" (the innermost part) is still firm.

5 ▲ Place a colander in the sink before the pasta has finished cooking. As soon as the pasta tastes done, tip it all into the colander (you may first want to reserve a cupful of the hot cooking water to add to the sauce if it needs thinning). Shake the colander lightly to remove most but not all of the cooking water. Pasta should never be over-drained.

6 ▲ Quickly turn the pasta into a warmed serving dish, and immediately toss it with a little butter or oil, or the prepared sauce. Alternatively, turn it into the cooking pan with the sauce, where it will be cooked for 1–2 minutes more as it is mixed into the sauce. Never allow pasta to sit undressed, as it will stick together and become unpalatable.

How to Cook Egg Pasta

Fresh egg pasta, especially home-made, cooks very much faster than dried pasta. Make sure everything is ready (the sauce, serving dishes, etc.) before you start boiling egg pasta, as there will not be time once the cooking starts, and egg pasta becomes soft and mushy very quickly.

1 Always cook pasta in a large pot with a generous amount of rapidly boiling water. Use at least 5 cups of water to a quantity of pasta made with 1 cup of flour. Salt the water as for dried pasta.

2 ▲ Drop the pasta into the boiling water all at once. Stir gently to prevent the pasta sticking to itself or to the pan. Cook the pasta at a fast boil.

3 ▲ Freshly made pasta can be done as little as 15 seconds after their cooking water comes back to a boil. Stuffed pasta takes a few minutes longer. When done, tip the pasta into the colander and proceed as for dried pasta.

Cannelloni with Tuna

Cannelloni sorpresa

Children love this pasta dish. Fontina cheese has a sweet, nutty flavor and melts perfectly.

Look for it at large supermarkets and Italian delicatessens.

Ingredients

1/4 cup butter
1/2 cup flour
about 3 3/4 cups hot milk
2 cans (7 oz each) tuna, drained
1 cup Fontina cheese, grated
1/4 tsp grated nutmeg
12 cannelloni tubes
2/3 cup grated Parmesan cheese
salt and freshly ground black pepper
fresh herbs, to garnish

serves 4–6

1 ▲ Melt the butter in a heavy saucepan, add the flour and stir over low heat for 1–2 minutes. Remove the pan from the heat and gradually add 1 1/2 cups of the milk, beating vigorously after each addition. Return the pan to the heat and whisk for 1–2 minutes, until the sauce is very thick and smooth. Remove from the heat.

3 ▲ Gradually whisk the remaining milk into the rest of the sauce, then return to the heat and simmer, whisking constantly, until thickened. Add the grated Fontina and nutmeg, with salt and pepper to taste. Simmer for a few more minutes, stirring frequently. Pour about one-third of the sauce into a baking dish and spread to the corners.

4 ▲ Fill the cannelloni tubes with the tuna mixture, pushing it in with the handle of a teaspoon. Place the cannelloni in a single layer in the dish. Thin the remaining sauce with a little more milk if necessary, then pour it over the cannelloni. Sprinkle with Parmesan cheese and bake for 30 minutes or until golden. Serve hot, garnished with herbs.

2 ▲ Mix the drained tuna with about 1/2 cup of the warm white sauce in a bowl. Add salt and black pepper to taste. Preheat the oven to 350°F.

Seafood Lasagne

Lasagne alla marinara

Rich and creamy, this flavorful lasagne makes a good dinner party dish.

Ingredients

5 tbsp butter
1 lb monkfish fillets, skinned and diced small
8 oz large shrimp, shelled, deveined and roughly chopped
3 cups button mushrooms, chopped
3 tbsp flour
2 ¹/₂ cups hot milk
1¹/₄ cups heavy cream
1 can (14 oz) chopped tomatoes
2 tbsp shredded fresh basil
8 sheets no-cook lasagne
1 cup grated Parmesan cheese
salt and freshly ground black pepper
fresh herbs, to garnish

serves 6

1 ▲ Melt 1 tbsp of the butter in a large, deep sauté pan, add the monkfish and shrimp and sauté over medium to high heat for 2–3 minutes. As soon as the shrimp turn pink, remove them with a slotted spoon and place in a bowl.

2 Add the mushrooms to the pan and sauté for about 5 minutes, until the juices run and the mushrooms are soft. Remove with a slotted spoon and add to the fish in the bowl.

3 Melt the remaining butter in a saucepan, add the flour and stir over low heat for 1–2 minutes. Remove the pan from the heat and gradually whisk in the milk. Return to the heat and bring to a boil, whisking. Lower the heat and simmer for 2–3 minutes, whisking occasionally, until thick. Whisk in the cream and cook over low heat for 2 more minutes.

4 ▲ Remove the sauce from the heat and stir in the fish and mushroom mixture with all the juices that have collected in the bowl. Add salt to taste, and plenty of pepper. Preheat the oven to 375°F.

5 Spread half the chopped tomatoes over the bottom of a baking dish. Sprinkle with half the basil and add salt and pepper to taste. Ladle one-third of the sauce over the tomatoes.

6 ▲ Cover the sauce with four lasagne sheets. Spread the remaining tomatoes over the lasagne and sprinkle with the basil and salt and pepper to taste. Ladle half the sauce over. Arrange the remaining lasagne sheets on top, top with the remaining sauce and cover with the cheese. Bake for 30–40 minutes until golden and bubbling. Serve hot, garnished with fresh herbs.

Spaghetti with Clams and White Wine   *Spaghetti alle vongole*

Raid the pantry to make this quick and easy pasta dish with an intense flavor.

Ingredients
2 tbsp olive oil
1 onion, very finely chopped
2 garlic cloves, crushed
1 can (14 oz) chopped tomatoes
²/₃ cup dry white wine
1 jar or can (5 oz) clams in natural juice,
 drained with juice reserved
12 oz dried spaghetti
2 tbsp finely chopped fresh flat-leaf
 parsley, plus extra
 to garnish
salt and freshly ground black pepper
serves 4

Cook's Tip
The tomato sauce can be made several days ahead of time and kept in the refrigerator. Add the clams and heat them through at the last minute—but don't let the sauce boil or they will toughen.

1 Heat the oil in a saucepan, add the onion and cook gently, stirring frequently for about 5 minutes, until softened, but not brown.

2 ▲ Stir in the garlic, tomatoes, wine and reserved clam juice, with salt to taste. Add a generous grinding of black pepper. Bring to a boil, stirring, then lower the heat. Cover the pan and simmer the sauce gently for about 20 minutes, stirring occasionally.

3 ▲ Meanwhile, coil the spaghetti into a large saucepan of rapidly boiling salted water and cook for 12 minutes or until it is *al dente*.

4 Drain the spaghetti. Add the clams and finely chopped parsley to the tomato sauce and heat through, then taste for seasoning. Pour the drained spaghetti into a warmed serving bowl, pour on the tomato sauce and toss to mix. Serve immediately, sprinkled with more parsley.

Pasta with Cream and Parmesan   *Pasta Alfredo*

This popular classic originated in Rome. It is incredibly quick and simple, perfect for a midweek supper.

Ingredients
12 oz dried fettuccine
2 tbsp butter
1¼ cups heavy cream
²/₃ cup grated Parmesan cheese, plus
 extra to serve
2 tbsp finely chopped fresh flat-leaf
 parsley, plus extra
 to garnish
salt and freshly ground black pepper
serves 3–4

Variation
In Rome, fettuccine would traditionally be served with this sauce, but tagliatelle can be used if you prefer. Pasta shapes, such as penne, rigatoni or farfalle, are also suitable.

1 Cook the fettuccine in a large pan of rapidly boiling salted water for 8–10 minutes or until *al dente*.

2 ▲ Meanwhile, melt the butter in a large flameproof casserole and add the cream and Parmesan, with salt and pepper to taste. Stir over medium heat until the cheese has melted and the sauce has thickened.

3 ▲ Drain the fettuccine and add it to the sauce with the chopped parsley. Fold the pasta and sauce together over medium heat until the strands of pasta are generously coated. Grind more black pepper over the pasta and garnish with the extra chopped parsley. Serve immediately, with a bowl of grated Parmesan served separately.

Tagliatelle with Bolognese Sauce   *Tagliatelle alla bolognese*

Most people think of Bolognese sauce, the famous ragù from Bologna, as being served with spaghetti. Traditionally, it is served with tagliatelle.

Ingredients

2 tbsp olive oil
1 onion, finely chopped
1 carrot, finely chopped
1 celery stick, finely chopped
1 garlic clove, crushed
12 oz ground beef
⅔ cup red wine
1 cup milk
1 can (14 oz) chopped tomatoes
1 tbsp sun-dried tomato paste
12 oz dried tagliatelle
salt and freshly ground black pepper
shredded fresh basil, to garnish
grated Parmesan cheese, to serve

serves 4

1 ▲ Heat the oil in a large saucepan. Add the onion, carrot, celery and garlic and cook gently, stirring frequently, for about 10 minutes, until softened. Do not let the vegetables color.

2 ▲ Add the ground beef to the pan with the vegetables and cook over medium heat until the meat changes color, stirring constantly and breaking up any lumps with a wooden spoon.

3 ▲ Pour in the wine. Stir frequently until it has evaporated, then add the milk and continue cooking and stirring until this has evaporated, too.

Cook's Tip

Don't skimp on the cooking time— it is essential for a full-flavored Bolognese sauce. Some Italian cooks insist on cooking it for 3–4 hours, so the longer the better.

4 ▲ Stir in the tomatoes and tomato paste, with salt and pepper to taste. Simmer the sauce uncovered, over the lowest possible heat for at least 45 minutes.

5 Cook the tagliatelle in a large pan of rapidly boiling salted water for 8–10 minutes or until *al dente*. Drain thoroughly and pour into a warmed large bowl. Pour on the sauce and toss to combine. Garnish with basil and serve immediately, with Parmesan cheese served separately.

Penne with Pancetta and Cream

Penne alla carbonara

This makes a gloriously rich supper dish. Follow it with a simple salad.

Ingredients

12 oz dried penne
2 tbsp olive oil
1 small onion, finely chopped
6 oz pancetta slices, any rinds removed,
    cut into bite-size strips
1–2 garlic cloves, crushed
5 egg yolks
³/₄ cup heavy cream
1¹/₃ cups grated Parmesan cheese, plus
    extra to serve
salt and freshly ground black pepper

serves 3–4

1 ▲ Cook the penne in a large pan of rapidly boiling salted water for about 10 minutes or until *al dente*.

2 Meanwhile, heat the oil in a large flameproof casserole. Add the onion and cook gently for about 5 minutes, stirring frequently, until softened. Add the pancetta and garlic. Cook over medium heat until the pancetta is cooked but not crisp. Remove the pan from the heat and set aside.

3 ▲ Put the egg yolks in a bowl and add the cream and Parmesan cheese. Grind in plenty of black pepper. Beat well to mix.

4 ▲ Drain the penne thoroughly, pour into the casserole and toss over medium to high heat until the pancetta mixture is evenly mixed with the pasta.

5 Remove from the heat, pour in the egg yolk mixture and toss well to combine. Spoon into a large shallow serving dish, grind a little black pepper on top and sprinkle with some of the extra Parmesan. Serve the rest of the Parmesan separately.

Cook's Tip

Serve this dish the moment it is ready or it will not be hot enough. Having added the egg yolks, don't return the pan to the heat or attempt to reheat the pasta and sauce together or the egg yolks will scramble and give the pasta a curdled appearance.

Three-cheese Lasagne

Lasagne ai tre formaggi

The cheese makes this lasagne quite expensive, so reserve it for a special occasion.

Ingredients

2 tbsp olive oil
1 onion, finely chopped
1 carrot, finely chopped
1 celery stalk, finely chopped
1 garlic clove, crushed
1½ lb ground beef
1 can (14 oz) chopped tomatoes
1¼ cups beef stock
1¼ cups red wine
2 tbsp sun-dried tomato paste
2 tsp dried oregano
9 sheets no-cook lasagne
3 5-oz packages mozzarella cheese,
    thinly sliced
2 cups ricotta cheese
4 oz Parmesan cheese, grated
salt and freshly ground black pepper
serves 6–8

1 Heat the oil and gently cook the onion, carrot, celery and garlic, stirring for 10 minutes until softened.

2 Add the beef and cook until it changes color, stirring constantly and breaking up the meat.

3 ▲ Add the tomatoes, stock, wine, tomato paste, oregano and salt and pepper and bring to a boil, stirring. Cover, lower the heat and simmer gently for 1 hour, stirring occasionally.

4 ▲ Preheat the oven to 375°F. Check for seasoning, then ladle one-third of the meat sauce into a 9 x 13 in baking dish and cover with 3 sheets of lasagne. Arrange one-third of the mozzarella slices over the top, dot with one-third of the ricotta, then sprinkle with one-third of the Parmesan.

5 Repeat these layers twice, then bake for 40 minutes. Let cool for 10 minutes before serving.

Tortiglioni with Spicy Sausage Sauce

Tortiglioni alla siciliana

This heady pasta dish is not for the faint-hearted. Serve it with a robust Sicilian red wine.

Ingredients

2 tbsp olive oil
1 onion, finely chopped
1 celery stalk, finely chopped
2 large garlic cloves, crushed
1 fresh red chili, seeded and chopped
1 lb ripe Italian plum tomatoes, peeled
    and finely chopped
2 tbsp tomato paste
⅔ cup red wine
1 tsp sugar
12 oz dried tortiglioni
6 oz spicy salami, rind removed
salt and freshly ground black pepper
2 tbsp chopped fresh parsley, to garnish
grated Parmesan cheese, to serve
serves 4

Cook's Tip

Buy the salami for this dish in one piece so that you can chop it into large chunks.

1 ▲ Heat the oil, then add the onion, celery, garlic and chili and cook gently, stirring frequently, for about 10 minutes, until softened.

2 Add the tomatoes, tomato paste, wine, sugar and salt and pepper to taste and bring to a boil, stirring. Lower the heat, cover and simmer gently, stirring occasionally, for about 20 minutes. Add a few spoonfuls of water occasionally if the sauce becomes too thick.

3 ▲ Meanwhile, drop the pasta into a large saucepan of rapidly boiling salted water and simmer, uncovered, for 10–12 minutes.

4 Chop the salami into bite-size chunks and add to the sauce. Heat through, then taste for seasoning.

5 Drain the pasta, tip it into a large bowl, then pour on the sauce and toss to mix. Scatter over the parsley and serve with grated Parmesan.

Pasta and Bolognese Casserole

Pasticcio

Pasticcio is Italian for pie, and in some regions this is made with a pastry topping. This simple version makes a great family supper because it's such a favorite with children.

Ingredients

8 oz dried conchiglie
1 quantity hot Bolognese Sauce (see Tagliatelle with Bolognese Sauce, page 38)
salt and freshly ground black pepper

For the white sauce

4 tbsp butter
1/2 cup flour
3 cups milk
1 cup grated Parmesan cheese
1 egg, beaten
good pinch of grated nutmeg
mixed salad leaves, to serve

serves 4

1 Cook the conchiglie in a large pan of rapidly boiling salted water for 10–12 minutes or until *al dente*.

2 Meanwhile, make the white sauce. Melt the butter in a saucepan until foaming, add the flour and stir over low heat for 1–2 minutes. Remove the pan from the heat and gradually whisk in the milk. Return the pan to the heat and bring to a boil, whisking constantly. Lower the heat and simmer for 2–3 minutes, whisking occasionally, until the sauce thickens. Remove the pan from the heat.

3 ▲ Preheat the oven to 375°F. Drain the pasta thoroughly, pour it into a 8 x 12-in baking dish and mix in the hot bolognese sauce. Level the surface.

4 ▲ Stir about two-thirds of the Parmesan into the white sauce, then stir in the beaten egg and nutmeg, with salt and pepper to taste. Pour on top of the pasta and sauce and sprinkle with the remaining Parmesan. Bake for 20 minutes or until golden and bubbling. Serve hot, straight from the dish. Add a salad garnish to each plate.

Cook's Tip

This is a good way of using up leftover bolognese sauce and cooked pasta—the quantities do not need to be exact.

Pasta with Eggplants

Pasta alla Norma

This Sicilian recipe is traditionally made from fried eggplants. This version is lighter.

Ingredients

2 medium eggplants, about 8 oz each,
   diced small
3 tbsp olive oil
10 oz dried macaroni or fusilli
2/3 cup grated Pecorino cheese
salt and freshly ground black pepper
shredded fresh basil leaves, to garnish
crusty bread, to serve

For the tomato sauce

2 tbsp olive oil
1 onion, finely chopped
1 can (14 oz) chopped tomatoes or
   1 jar (14 oz) passata
serves 4

Cook's Tip

In Sicily, a cheese called ricotta salata is used for this recipe. This is a matured salted ricotta that is grated like Pecorino and Parmesan. It is unlikely that you will find ricotta salata outside Sicily; Pecorino is the best substitute because it tastes slightly saltier than Parmesan.

1 Soak the diced eggplant in a bowl of cold salted water for 30 minutes.

2 Meanwhile, preheat the oven to 425°F. Make the sauce. Heat the oil in a large saucepan, add the onion and cook gently for about 3 minutes, until softened. Add the tomatoes, with salt and pepper to taste. Bring to a boil, lower the heat, cover and simmer for 20 minutes. Stir the sauce and add a few spoonfuls of water occasionally, to prevent it from becoming too thick. Remove from the heat.

3 ▲ Drain the eggplants and pat dry. Spread the pieces out in a roasting pan, add the oil and toss to coat. Bake for 20–25 minutes, turning the eggplants every 4–5 minutes with a spatula so that they brown evenly.

4 Cook the pasta in a large pan of rapidly boiling salted water for 10–12 minutes or until *al dente*. Reheat the tomato sauce.

5 ▲ Drain the pasta thoroughly and add it to the tomato sauce, with half the roasted eggplant and half the Pecorino. Toss to mix, then taste for seasoning.

6 Spoon the pasta and sauce mixture into a warmed large serving dish and top with the remaining roasted eggplant. Scatter the shredded fresh basil leaves on top, followed by the remaining Pecorino. Serve immediately, with generous chunks of crusty bread.

Spinach and Ricotta Gnocchi
Gnocchi di spinaci e ricotta

The mixture for these tasty little herb dumplings needs to be handled very carefully to achieve light and fluffy results. Serve with sage butter and grated Parmesan.

Ingredients

6 garlic cloves, unpeeled
1 oz mixed fresh herbs, such as parsley,
    basil, thyme, coriander and chives,
    finely chopped
8 oz fresh spinach leaves
generous 1 cup ricotta cheese
1 egg yolk
⅔ cup grated Parmesan cheese
⅔ cup flour
¼ cup butter
2 tbsp fresh sage, chopped
salt and freshly ground black pepper
serves 4

1 Cook the garlic cloves in boiling water for 4 minutes. Drain and pop out of the skins. Place in a food processor with the herbs and blend to a purée or mash the garlic with a fork and add the herbs to mix well.

2 ▲ Place the spinach in a large pan with just the water that clings to the leaves and cook gently until wilted. Let cool, then squeeze out as much liquid as possible. Chop finely.

3 Place the ricotta in a bowl and beat in the egg yolk, spinach, herbs and garlic. Stir in half the Parmesan, sift in the flour and mix well.

Cook's Tip

Squeeze the spinach dry to ensure the gnocchi are not wet and to give a lighter result. The mixture should be fairly soft and will be easier to handle if chilled for an hour before preparing the dumplings.

4 ▲ Using floured hands, break off pieces of the mixture slightly smaller than a walnut and roll into small dumplings.

5 Bring a large pan of salted water to a boil and carefully add the gnocchi. When they rise to the top of the pan they are cooked. This should take about 3 minutes.

6 ▲ The gnocchi should be light and fluffy all the way through. If not, simmer for another minute. Drain well. Meanwhile, melt the butter in a frying pan and add the sage. Simmer gently for 1 minute. Add the gnocchi to the frying pan and toss in the butter over gentle heat for 1 minute, then serve sprinkled with the remaining Parmesan.

Gnocchi with Gorgonzola Sauce

Gnocchi al gorgonzola

Gnocchi are prepared all over Italy with different ingredients used in different regions.

These are gnocchi di patate, *potato dumplings.*

Ingredients

1 lb potatoes, unpeeled
1 large egg
1 cup flour
salt and freshly ground black pepper
fresh thyme sprigs, to garnish

For the sauce

4 oz Gorgonzola cheese
¼ cup heavy cream
1 tbsp fresh thyme, chopped
¼ cup freshly grated
    Parmesan cheese, to serve

serves 4

1 Cook the potatoes in boiling salted water for about 20 minutes until they are tender. Drain and, when cool enough to handle, remove the skins.

2 ▲ Force the potatoes through a sieve, pressing through using the back of a spoon, into a mixing bowl. Add plenty of seasoning and then beat in the egg until completely incorporated. Add the flour a little at a time, stirring well with a wooden spoon after each addition until you have a smooth dough. (You may not need all the flour.)

3 Turn the dough out onto a floured surface and knead for about 3 minutes, adding more flour if necessary, until it is smooth and soft and not sticky to the touch.

Cook's Tips

Choose dry, floury potatoes. Avoid new or red-skinned potatoes, which do not have the right dry texture.

4 ▲ Divide the dough into 6 equal pieces. Flour your hands and gently roll each piece between your hands into a log shape measuring 6–8 in long and 1 in around. Cut each log into 6–8 pieces, about 1 in long, then gently roll each piece in the flour. Form into gnocchi by gently pressing each piece on to the floured surface with the tines of a fork to leave ridges in the dough.

5 ▲ To cook, drop the gnocchi into a pan of boiling water about 12 at a time. Once they rise to the surface, after about 2 minutes, cook for 4–5 more minutes. Remove and drain.

6 Place the Gorgonzola, cream and thyme in a large frying pan and heat gently until the cheese melts to form a thick, creamy consistency. Add the drained gnocchi and toss well to combine. Serve with Parmesan and garnish with thyme.

Rice, Polenta & Pizzas

....

In the north of Italy, rice is served as a first course, as a creamy risotto, but you can serve it as a main dish, with a salad and Italian bread. Polenta, also from the north of Italy, is most often served with the main course, especially with meaty casseroles. Pizzas hail from the south, where they are eaten at any time of day, the ultimate convenience food.

Risotto with Spring Vegetables

Risotto primavera

This is one of the prettiest risottos, especially when made with yellow summer squash.

Ingredients

1 cup shelled fresh peas
1 cup green beans, cut into
 short lengths
2 tbsps olive oil
6 tbsp butter
2 small yellow summer squash, cut
 into matchsticks
1 onion, finely chopped
1½ cups risotto rice
½ cup Italian dry
 white vermouth
about 4 cups boiling chicken stock
1 cup grated Parmesan cheese
a small handful of fresh basil leaves,
 finely shredded, plus a few whole
 leaves, to garnish
salt and freshly ground black pepper

serves 4

1 Blanch the peas and beans in a large saucepan of lightly salted boiling water for 2–3 minutes, until just tender. Drain, refresh under cold running water, drain again and set aside for later.

2 ▲ Heat the oil and 2 tbsp of the butter in a medium saucepan until foaming. Add the squash and cook gently for 2–3 minutes or until just softened. Remove with a slotted spoon and set aside. Add the onion to the pan and cook gently for about 3 minutes, stirring frequently, until softened.

3 ▲ Stir in the rice until the grains start to swell and burst, then add the vermouth. Stir until the vermouth stops sizzling and most of it has been absorbed by the rice, then add a few ladlefuls of the stock, with salt and pepper to taste. Stir over low heat until the stock has been absorbed.

4 Continue cooking and stirring for 20–25 minutes, adding the remaining stock a few ladlefuls at a time. The rice should be *al dente* and the risotto should have a moist and creamy appearance.

5 ▲ Gently stir in the vegetables, the remaining butter and about half the grated Parmesan. Heat through, then stir in the shredded basil and taste for seasoning. Garnish with a few whole basil leaves and serve hot, with the remaining grated Parmesan served separately.

Variations

Shelled fava beans can be used instead of the peas, and asparagus tips instead of the green beans. Use green zucchini if yellow summer squash are unavailable.

Rice with Peas, Ham and Cheese

Risi e bisi

A classic risotto from the Veneto. Although it is traditionally served as an appetizer in

Italy, risi e bisi makes an excellent supper dish with hot crusty bread.

Ingredients

6 tbsp butter
1 small onion, finely chopped
about 4 cups boiling
   chicken stock
1¹/₂ cups risotto rice
²/₃ cup dry white wine
2 cups frozen peas, thawed
4 oz cooked ham, diced
salt and freshly ground black pepper
²/₃ cup Parmesan cheese,
   to serve

serves 4

1 ▲ Melt 4 tbsp of the butter in a saucepan until foaming. Add the onion and cook gently for about 3 minutes, stirring frequently, until softened. Have the hot stock ready in an adjacent pan.

2 ▲ Add the rice to the onion mixture. Stir until the grains start to burst, then pour in the wine. Stir until it stops sizzling and most of it has been absorbed, then pour in a little hot stock, with salt and pepper to taste. Stir over low heat until the stock has been absorbed.

3 ▲ Add the remaining stock, a little at a time, allowing the rice to absorb all the liquid before adding more, and stirring constantly. Add the peas toward the end. After 20–25 minutes, the rice should be *al dente* and the risotto moist and creamy.

4 ▲ Gently stir in the diced cooked ham and the remaining butter. Heat through until the butter has melted, then taste for seasoning. Transfer to a warmed serving bowl. Grate or shave a little Parmesan over the top and serve the rest separately.

Risotto with Four Cheeses

Risotto ai quattro formaggi

This is a very rich dish. Serve it for a dinner-party first course, with sparkling white wine.

Ingredients

3 tbsp butter
1 small onion, finely chopped
4 cups boiling chicken stock
1¾ cups risotto rice
scant 1 cup sparkling dry white wine
½ cup grated Gruyère cheese
½ cup Fontina cheese, diced small
½ cup Gorgonzola cheese, crumbled
⅔ cup grated Parmesan cheese
salt and freshly ground black pepper
fresh flat-leaf parsley, to garnish
serves 6

Cook's Tip
If you're feeling extravagant you can use Champagne for this risotto, although Asti spumante works quite well.

1 Melt the butter in a saucepan until foaming. Add the onion and cook gently, stirring frequently for about 3 minutes, until softened. Have the hot stock ready in an adjacent pan.

2 ▲ Add the rice and stir until the grains start to swell and burst, then add the sparkling wine. Stir until it stops sizzling and most of it has been absorbed by the rice, then pour in a little of the hot stock. Add salt and pepper to taste. Stir over low heat until the stock has been absorbed.

3 Add more stock, a little at a time, allowing the rice to absorb it before adding more, and stirring constantly. After 20–25 minutes the rice will be *al dente* and the risotto creamy.

4 ▲ Turn off the heat under the pan, then add the Gruyère, Fontina, Gorgonzola and 2 tbsp of the Parmesan. Stir gently until the cheeses have melted, then taste for seasoning. Pour into a serving bowl and garnish with parsley. Serve the remaining Parmesan separately.

Polenta with Mushroom Sauce

Polenta con salsa di funghi

Polenta, made from maize flour, fulfills the same function as rice, bread or potatoes in forming the starchy base for a meal. Here, it is cooked until it forms a soft dough, then flavored with Parmesan. Its subtle taste works well with the rich mushroom sauce.

Ingredients

5 cups vegetable stock
3 cups polenta
²/₃ cup grated Parmesan cheese
salt and freshly ground black pepper

For the sauce

1 cup dried porcini mushrooms
1 tbsp olive oil
4 tbsp butter
1 onion, finely chopped
1 carrot, finely chopped
1 celery stalk, finely chopped
2 garlic cloves, crushed
6 cups mixed chestnut and large flat
   mushrooms, roughly chopped
¹/₂ cup red wine
1 can (14 oz) chopped tomatoes
1 tsp tomato paste
1 tbsp chopped fresh thyme leaves
serves 4

1 ▲ Make the sauce. Put the dried mushrooms in a bowl, add ²/₃ cup of hot water and soak for 20 minutes. Drain the mushrooms, reserving the liquid, and chop them roughly.

2 Heat the oil and butter in a saucepan and add the onion, carrot, celery and garlic. Cook over low heat for about 5 minutes, until the vegetables are beginning to soften, then raise the heat and add the fresh and soaked dried mushrooms to the pan of vegetables. Cook for 8–10 minutes, until the mushrooms are softened and golden.

3 ▲ Pour in the wine and cook rapidly for 2–3 minutes, until reduced, then pour in the tomatoes and reserved mushroom liquid. Stir in the tomato paste with the thyme and plenty of salt and pepper. Lower the heat and simmer for 20 minutes, until the sauce is rich and thick.

Cook's Tip

The polenta will spit during cooking, so use a long-handled spoon and wrap a towel around your hand to protect it while stirring.

4 ▲ Meanwhile, heat the stock in a large heavy saucepan. Add a generous pinch of salt. As soon as it simmers, pour in the polenta in a fine stream, whisking until the mixture is smooth. Cook for 30 minutes, stirring constantly, until the polenta comes away from the pan. Remove from the heat and stir in half the Parmesan and some black pepper.

5 Divide among four heated bowls and top each with sauce. Sprinkle with the remaining Parmesan.

Butternut Squash and Sage Pizza

Pizza con zucca e salvia

The combination of the sweet butternut squash, sage and sharp goat cheese works wonderfully on this pizza. Pumpkin and winter squashes are popular in northern Italy.

Ingredients

1 tbsp butter
2 tbsp olive oil
2 shallots, finely chopped
1 butternut squash, peeled, seeded and cubed, about 1 pound prepared weight
16 sage leaves
1 recipe risen Pizza Dough
1 recipe Tomato Sauce
1 cup mozzarella cheese, sliced
¹/₂ cup firm goat cheese
salt and freshly ground black pepper

serves 4

1 ▲ Preheat the oven to 400°F. Oil four baking sheets. Put the butter and oil in a roasting pan and heat in the oven for a few minutes. Add the shallots, squash and half the sage leaves. Toss to coat. Roast for 15–20 minutes, until tender.

2 ▲ Raise the oven temperature to 425°F. Divide the pizza dough into four equal pieces and roll out each piece on a lightly floured surface to a 10-in round.

3 ▲ Transfer each round to a baking sheet and spread with the tomato sauce, leaving a ¹/₂-in border all around. Spoon the squash and shallot mixture over the crust.

4 ▲ Arrange the slices of mozzarella over the squash mixture and crumble the goat cheese on top. Scatter the remaining sage leaves on top and season with plenty of salt and pepper. Bake for 15–20 minutes, until the cheese has melted and the crust on each pizza is golden.

Ricotta and Fontina Pizza

Pizza con ricotta e fontina

The flavor of the earthy mixed mushrooms is delicious with the creamy cheeses.

Ingredients

For the pizza dough

½ tsp active dried yeast
pinch of sugar
4 cups flour
1 tsp salt
2 tbsp olive oil

For the tomato sauce

1 can (14 oz) chopped tomatoes
⅔ cup passata
1 large garlic clove, finely chopped
1 tsp dried oregano
1 bay leaf
2 tsp malt vinegar
salt and freshly ground black pepper

For the topping

2 tbsp olive oil
1 garlic clove, finely chopped
4 cups mixed mushrooms (chestnut, flat
 or button), sliced
2 tbsp chopped fresh oregano, plus
 whole leaves, to garnish
generous 1 cup ricotta cheese
8 oz Fontina cheese, sliced

**makes 4 10-in thin
 crust pizzas**

1 ▲ Make the dough. Put 1¼ cups warm water in a measuring cup. Add the yeast and sugar and set aside for 5–10 minutes until frothy. Sift the flour and salt into a large bowl and make a well in the center. Gradually pour in the yeast mixture and the olive oil. Mix to make a smooth dough. Knead on a lightly floured surface for about 10 minutes until smooth, springy and elastic. Place the dough in a floured bowl, cover and let rise in a warm place for 1½ hours.

2 Meanwhile, make the tomato sauce. Place all the ingredients in a saucepan, cover and bring to a boil. Lower the heat, remove the lid and simmer for 20 minutes, stirring occasionally, until reduced.

3 ▲ Make the topping. Heat the oil in a frying pan. Add the garlic and mushrooms, with salt and pepper to taste. Cook, stirring, for about 5 minutes or until the mushrooms are tender and golden. Set aside.

4 ▲ Preheat the oven to 425°F. Brush four baking sheets with oil. Knead the dough for 2 minutes, then divide into four equal pieces. Roll out each piece to a 10-in round and place on a baking sheet.

5 Spoon the tomato sauce over each dough round. Brush the edge with a little olive oil. Add the mushrooms, oregano and cheese. Bake for about 15 minutes until golden brown. Scatter the oregano leaves on top.

Fried Pizza Pasties

Panzerotti

These tasty little morsels are served all over central and southern Italy as a snack food or

as part of a hot antipasto. Although similar to calzone, they are fried instead of baked.

Ingredients
½ recipe Pizza Dough
½ recipe Tomato Sauce
8 oz mozzarella cheese, chopped
4 oz Italian salami, thinly sliced
handful of fresh basil leaves, roughly torn
sunflower oil, for deep frying
salt and freshly ground black pepper
serves 4

Cook's Tip
To test that the oil is ready, carefully drop a piece of bread into the oil. If it sizzles instantly, the oil is ready.

1 Preheat the oven to 400°F. Brush two baking sheets with oil. Divide the dough into 12 pieces and roll out each piece on a lightly floured surface to a 4-in round.

2 ▲ Spread the center of each round with a little of the tomato sauce, leaving a sufficient border all around for sealing the pasty, then top with a few pieces of mozzarella and salami slices. Sprinkle with salt and freshly ground black pepper and add a few fresh basil leaves to each round.

3 ▲ Brush the edges of the dough rounds with a little water, then fold over and press together to seal.

4 Heat oil to a depth of about 4 in in a heavy pan. When hot, deep-fry the pasties, a few at a time, for 8–10 minutes until golden. Drain on paper towels and serve hot.

Sicilian Pizza

Pizza alla siciliana

This robust-flavored pizza is topped with mozzarella and Pecorino cheeses.

Ingredients
1 small eggplant, cut into thin rounds
2 tbsp olive oil
½ recipe risen Pizza Dough
½ recipe Tomato Sauce
6 oz mozzarella cheese, sliced
½ cup pitted black olives
1 tbsp drained capers
¼ cup grated Pecorino cheese
salt and freshly ground black pepper
serves 2

Cook's Tip
For best results choose olives that have been marinated in extra virgin olive oil and flavored with herbs and garlic.

1 ▲ Preheat the oven to 400°F. Brush one or two baking sheets with oil. Brush the eggplant rounds with olive oil and arrange them on the baking sheet(s). Bake for 10–15 minutes, turning once, until browned and tender. Remove the eggplant slices from the baking sheet(s) and drain on paper towels.

2 Raise the oven temperature to 425°F. Roll out the pizza dough into two 10-in rounds. Transfer to baking sheets and spread with the tomato sauce.

3 ▲ Pile the eggplant slices on top of the tomato sauce and cover with the mozzarella. Dot with the black olives and capers. Sprinkle the Pecorino cheese liberally over the top, and season with plenty of salt and pepper. Bake for 15–20 minutes, until the crust on each pizza is golden.

Fish & Shellfish

....

Italy has such an extensive coastline—and so many lakes, rivers and streams—that it is no wonder that fish and shellfish are so popular. Of course there are many different types that are unique to the country itself, but the most common varieties are available outside Italy. Cooking methods are very simple and quick, and any accompanying sauces light and fresh.

Monkfish with Tomato and Olive Sauce   *Pesce alla calabrese*

This dish comes from the coast of Calabria in southern Italy. Garlic-flavored mashed

potatoes are delicious with its robust sauce.

Ingredients

1 lb fresh mussels, scrubbed
a few fresh basil sprigs
2 garlic cloves, roughly chopped
1¼ cups dry white wine
2 tbsp olive oil
1 tbsp butter
2 lb monkfish fillets, skinned and cut into
    large chunks
1 onion, finely chopped
1¼ lb jar sugocasa or passata
1 tbsp sun-dried tomato paste
1 cup pitted black olives
salt and freshly ground black pepper
extra fresh basil leaves, to garnish

serves 4

1 ▲ Put the mussels in a flameproof casserole with some basil leaves, the garlic and the wine. Cover and bring to a boil. Lower the heat and simmer for 5 minutes, shaking the pan frequently. Remove the mussels, discarding any that fail to open. Strain the cooking liquid and reserve.

2 ▲ Heat the oil and butter until foaming, add the monkfish pieces and sauté over a medium heat until they just change color. Remove.

3 ▲ Add the onion to the juices in the casserole and cook gently for about 5 minutes, stirring frequently, until softened. Add the sugocasa or passata, the reserved cooking liquid from the mussels and the tomato paste. Season with salt and pepper to taste. Bring to a boil, stirring, then lower the heat, cover and simmer for 20 minutes, stirring occasionally.

4 ▲ Pull off and discard the top shells from the mussels. Add the monkfish pieces to the tomato sauce and cook gently for 5 minutes. Gently stir in the olives and remaining basil, then taste for seasoning. Place the mussels in their half shells on top of the sauce, cover the pan and heat the mussels through for 1–2 minutes. Serve immediately, garnished with basil.

Char-grilled Squid

Grigliata di calamari

If you like your food hot, chop some—or all—of the chili seeds with the flesh. If not, cut the chilies in half lengthwise, scrape out the seeds and discard them before chopping the flesh.

Ingredients

2 whole prepared squid, with tentacles
5 tbsp olive oil
2 tbsp balsamic vinegar
2 fresh red chilies, finely chopped
¼ cup dry white wine
salt and freshly ground black pepper
hot cooked risotto rice, to serve
sprigs of fresh parsley, to garnish

serves 2

3 ▲ Cut the squid bodies into diagonal strips. Pile the hot risotto rice in the center of heated soup plates and top with the strips of squid, arranging them in criss-cross fashion. Keep hot.

4 ▲ Add the chopped tentacles and chilies to the pan and toss over medium heat for 2 minutes. Stir in the wine, then drizzle over the squid and rice. Garnish with the parsley and serve immediately.

1 ▲ Make a lengthwise cut down the body of each squid, then open out the body flat. Score the flesh on both sides of the bodies in a criss-cross pattern with the tip of a sharp knife. Chop the tentacles. Place all the squid in a china or glass dish. Whisk the oil and vinegar in a small bowl. Add salt and pepper to taste and pour over the squid. Cover and let marinate for about 1 hour.

2 ▲ Heat a ridged cast-iron pan until hot. Add the body of one of the squid. Cook over medium heat for 2–3 minutes, pressing the squid with a spatula to keep it flat. Repeat on the other side. Cook the other squid body in the same way.

Pan-fried Shrimp in their Shells

Gamberi fritti in padella

Although expensive, this is a very quick and simple dish, ideal for an impromptu supper with friends. Serve with hot crusty Italian bread to scoop up the juices.

Ingredients
¼ cup extra virgin olive oil
32 large fresh shrimp, in their shells
4 garlic cloves, finely chopped
½ cup Italian dry white vermouth
3 tbsp passata
salt and freshly ground black pepper
chopped fresh flat-leaf parsley, to garnish
crusty bread, to serve
serves 4

Cook's Tip
Shrimp in their shells are sweet and juicy, and fun to eat with your fingers. They can be quite messy though, so provide guests with finger bowls and napkins.

1 ▲ Heat the olive oil in a large heavy frying pan until just sizzling. Add the shrimp and toss over medium to high heat until their shells just begin to turn pink. Sprinkle the garlic over the shrimp in the pan and toss again, then add the vermouth and let it bubble, tossing the shrimp constantly so that they cook evenly and absorb the flavors of the garlic and vermouth.

2 ▲ Keeping the pan on the heat, add the passata, with salt and pepper to taste. Stir until the shrimp are thoroughly coated in the sauce. Serve immediately, sprinkled with the parsley and accompanied by plenty of hot crusty bread.

Broiled Red Mullet with Rosemary

Triglie al rosmarino

This recipe is very simple—the taste of broiled red mullet is so good in itself that it needs very little to bring out the flavor.

Ingredients
4 red mullet, cleaned, about
    10 oz each
4 garlic cloves, cut lengthwise into
    thin slivers
5 tbsp olive oil
2 tbsp balsamic vinegar
2 tsp very finely chopped fresh rosemary
    or 1 tsp dried rosemary
freshly ground black pepper
coarse sea salt, to serve
fresh rosemary sprigs and lemon
    wedges, to garnish
serves 4

Variation
Red mullet are extra delicious cooked on the barbecue. If possible, enclose them in a basket grill so that they are easy to turn over.

1 ▲ Cut three diagonal slits in both sides of each fish. Push the garlic slivers into the slits. Place the fish in a single layer in a shallow dish. Whisk the oil, vinegar and rosemary, with ground black pepper to taste.

2 ▲ Pour the marinade over the fish, cover with plastic wrap and let marinate in a cool place for 1 hour. Put the fish on the rack of a broiler pan and broil for 5–6 minutes on each side, turning once and brushing with the marinade. Serve hot, sprinkled with coarse sea salt and garnished with fresh rosemary sprigs and lemon wedges.

Pan-fried Sole with Lemon

Sogliole al limone

The delicate flavor and texture of sole is brought out in this simple, classic recipe. Lemon sole is used here because it is easier to obtain—and less expensive—than Dover sole.

Ingredients

2–3 tbsp flour
4 lemon sole fillets
3 tbsp olive oil
4 tbsp butter
$\frac{1}{4}$ cup lemon juice
2 tbsp rinsed bottled capers
salt and freshly ground black pepper
fresh flat-leaf parsley and lemon wedges,
    to garnish

serves 2

Cook's Tip

It is important to cook the pan juices to the right color after removing the fish. Too pale, and they will taste insipid, too dark, and they may taste bitter. Take great care not to be distracted at this point so that you can watch the color of the juices change to a golden brown.

1 ▲ Season the flour with salt and black pepper. Coat the sole fillets evenly on both sides. Heat the oil with half the butter in a large shallow pan until foaming. Add two sole fillets and fry over medium heat for 2–3 minutes on each side.

2 Lift out the sole fillets with a spatula and place on a warmed serving platter. Keep hot. Fry the remaining sole fillets.

3 ▲ Remove the pan from the heat and add the lemon juice and remaining butter. Return the pan to high heat and stir vigorously until the pan juices are sizzling and beginning to turn golden brown. Remove from the heat and stir in the capers.

4 Pour the pan juices over the sole, sprinkle with salt and pepper to taste and garnish with the parsley. Add the lemon wedges and serve immediately.

Three-color Fish Kebabs

Spiedini tricolore

Don't let the fish marinate for more than an hour. The lemon juice will start to break down the fibers of the fish after this time and it will be difficult not to overcook it.

Ingredients

½ cup olive oil
finely grated rind and juice of
1 large lemon
1 tsp crushed chili flakes
12 oz monkfish fillet, cubed
12 oz swordfish fillet, cubed
12 oz thick salmon fillet or
steak, cubed
2 red, yellow or orange bell peppers,
cored, seeded and cut into squares
2 tbsp finely chopped fresh
flat-leaf parsley
salt and freshly ground black pepper

For the sweet tomato and
chili salsa

8 oz ripe tomatoes, finely chopped
1 garlic clove, crushed
1 fresh red chili, seeded and chopped
3 tbsp extra virgin olive oil
1 tbsp lemon juice
1 tbsp finely chopped fresh
flat-leaf parsley
pinch of sugar
serves 4

1 ▲ Put the oil in a shallow glass or china bowl and add the lemon rind and juice, the chili flakes and pepper to taste. Whisk to combine, then add the fish chunks. Turn to coat evenly.

2 Add the pepper squares, stir, then cover and marinate in a cool place for 1 hour, turning occasionally.

Variation

Use tuna instead of swordfish. It has a similar meaty texture.

3 ▲ Thread the fish and peppers onto eight oiled metal skewers, reserving the marinade. Barbecue or grill the skewered fish for 5–8 minutes, turning once.

4 Meanwhile, make the salsa by mixing all the ingredients in a bowl, and seasoning to taste with salt and pepper. Heat the reserved marinade in a small pan, remove from the heat and stir in the parsley, with salt and pepper to taste. Serve the kebabs hot, with the marinade spooned over, accompanied by the salsa.

Roast Sea Bass

Branzino al forno

Sea bass has meaty flesh. It is an expensive fish, best cooked as simply as possible. Avoid elaborate sauces, which would mask its delicate flavor.

Ingredients

1 fennel bulb with fronds, about 10 oz
2 lemons
½ cup olive oil
1 small red onion, diced
2 sea bass, about 1¼ lb each, cleaned
    with heads left on
½ cup dry white wine
salt and freshly ground black pepper
lemon slices, to garnish

serves 4

1 ▲ Preheat the oven to 375°F. Cut the fronds off the top of the fennel and reserve for the garnish. Cut the fennel bulb lengthwise into thin wedges, then into dice. Cut one half lemon into four slices. Squeeze the juice from the remaining lemon half and the other lemon.

2 ▲ Heat 2 tbsp of the oil in a frying pan, add the diced fennel and onion and cook gently, stirring frequently, for about 5 minutes, until softened. Remove from the heat.

3 ▲ Make three diagonal slashes on both sides of each sea bass with a sharp knife. Brush a roasting pan generously with oil, add the fish and tuck two lemon slices in each cavity. Scatter the softened fennel and onion over the fish.

Cook's Tip

Farmed or wild sea bass are available year round from the fishmonger. They are expensive, but well worth buying for a special main course. Sizes vary from the ones used here, which are a very good size for two servings, to 3–4½ lb, which take up to 50 minutes to cook.

4 ▲ Whisk the remaining oil, the lemon juice and salt and pepper to taste and pour over the fish. Cover with foil and roast for 30 minutes or until the flesh flakes, removing the foil for the last 10 minutes. Discard the lemon slices, transfer the fish to a heated serving platter and keep hot.

5 Put the roasting pan on top of the stove. Add the wine and stir over medium heat to incorporate all the pan juices. Bring to a boil, then spoon the juices over the fish. Garnish with the reserved fennel fronds and lemon slices and serve immediately.

Stuffed Swordfish Rolls

Involtini di pesce spada

This is a very tasty dish, with strong flavors from the tomato, olive and caper sauce—and from the salty Pecorino cheese. If desired, substitute Parmesan cheese, which is milder.

Ingredients

2 tbsp olive oil
1 small onion, finely chopped
1 celery stalk, finely chopped
1 lb ripe Italian plum
   tomatoes, chopped
4 oz pitted green olives, half roughly
   chopped, half left whole
3 tbsp drained bottled capers
4 large swordfish steaks, each about
   $\frac{1}{2}$ in thick and 4 oz in weight
1 egg
$\frac{2}{3}$ cup grated Pecorino cheese
$\frac{1}{2}$ cup fresh white bread crumbs
salt and freshly ground black pepper
sprigs of fresh parsley, to garnish
serves 4

Cook's Tip

This dish is not for the inexperienced cook because the pounding, stuffing and rolling of the fish is quite tricky. If you prefer, you can omit the stuffing and simply cook the swordfish steaks in the sauce.

1 ▲ Heat the oil in a large heavy frying pan. Add the onion and celery and cook gently for about 3 minutes, stirring frequently. Stir in the tomatoes, olives and capers, with salt and pepper to taste. Bring to a boil, then lower the heat, cover and simmer for about 15 minutes. Stir occasionally and add a little water if the sauce becomes too thick.

2 Remove the fish skin and place each steak between two sheets of plastic wrap. Pound lightly with a rolling pin until each steak is reduced to about $\frac{1}{4}$ in thick.

3 ▲ Beat the egg in a bowl and add the cheese, bread crumbs and a few spoonfuls of the sauce. Stir well to mix to a moist stuffing. Spread one-quarter of the stuffing over each swordfish steak, then roll up into a sausage shape. Secure with wooden toothpicks.

4 ▲ Add the rolls to the sauce in the pan and bring to a boil. Lower the heat, cover and simmer for about 30 minutes, turning once. Add a little water as the sauce reduces.

5 Remove the rolls from the sauce and discard the toothpicks. Place on warmed dinner plates and spoon the sauce over and around. Garnish with the parsley and serve hot.

Poultry & Meat

························

*The Italians eat a wide variety of different meats,
and tastes vary according to region. Veal, pork and
poultry are popular all over the country, while beef
is farmed and eaten more in the north, and lamb is
a great Roman speciality. All meats are eaten as a
second course—*secondo piatto—*usually simple
and served solo, with vegetables to follow.*

Beef Stew with Tomatoes, Wine and Peas *Spezzatino*

It seems there are as many spezzatino recipes as there are Italian cooks. This one is very traditional, perfect for a winter lunch or dinner. Serve it with boiled or mashed potatoes to soak up the deliciously rich sauce.

Ingredients

2 tbsp flour
2 tsp chopped fresh thyme or
    1 tsp dried thyme
2¼ lb braising or stewing steak, cut into
    large cubes
3 tbsp olive oil
1 medium onion, roughly chopped
1 jar (1 lb) sugocasa or passata
1 cup beef stock
1 cup red wine
2 garlic cloves, crushed
2 tbsp tomato paste
2 cups shelled fresh peas
1 tsp sugar
salt and freshly ground black pepper
fresh thyme, to garnish

serves 4

1 ▲ Preheat the oven to 325°F. Put the flour in a shallow dish and season with the thyme and salt and pepper. Add the beef cubes and coat evenly.

2 ▲ Heat the oil in a large flameproof casserole, add the beef and brown on all sides over medium to high heat. Remove with a slotted spoon and drain on paper towels.

3 ▲ Add the onion to the pan, scraping the base of the pan to mix in any sediment. Cook gently for about 3 minutes, stirring frequently, until softened, then stir in the sugocasa, stock, wine, garlic and tomato paste. Bring to a boil, stirring. Return the beef to the pan and stir well to coat with the sauce. Cover and cook in the oven for 1½ hours.

4 ▲ Stir in the peas and sugar. Return the casserole to the oven and cook for 30 more minutes, or until the beef is tender. Taste for seasoning. Garnish with fresh thyme before serving.

Variation

Use thawed frozen peas instead of fresh. Add them 10 minutes before the end of cooking.

Meatballs with Peperonata

Polpette di manzo

These taste very good with creamed potatoes. Use a potato ricer to get them really smooth.

Ingredients

14 oz ground beef
2 cups fresh white bread crumbs
²/₃ cup grated Parmesan cheese
2 eggs, beaten
pinch of paprika
pinch of grated nutmeg
1 tsp dried mixed herbs
2 thin slices of mortadella or prosciutto
    (total weight about 2 oz), chopped
vegetable oil, for shallow frying
salt and freshly ground black pepper
snipped fresh basil leaves,
    to garnish

For the peperonata

2 tbsp olive oil
1 small onion, thinly sliced
2 yellow bell peppers, cored, seeded and
    cut lengthwise into thin strips
2 red bell peppers, cored, seeded and
    cut lengthwise into thin strips
1¹/₄ cups finely chopped tomatoes
    or passata
1 tbsp chopped fresh parsley
serves 4

1 ▲ Put the ground beef in a bowl. Add half the bread crumbs and all the remaining ingredients, including salt and ground black pepper to taste. Mix well with clean wet hands. Divide the mixture into 12 equal portions and roll each into a ball. Flatten the meat balls slightly so they are about ¹/₂ in thick.

2 Put the remaining bread crumbs on a plate and roll the meatballs in them, a few at a time, until they are evenly coated. Place on a plate, cover with plastic wrap and chill for about 30 minutes to firm up.

3 ▲ Meanwhile, make the peperonata. Heat the oil in a medium saucepan, add the onion and cook gently for about 3 minutes, stirring frequently, until softened. Add the pepper strips and cook for 3 minutes, stirring constantly. Stir in the tomatoes and parsley, with salt and pepper to taste. Bring to a boil, stirring. Cover and cook for 15 minutes, then remove the lid and continue to cook, stirring frequently, for 10 more minutes, or until reduced and thick. Taste for seasoning. Keep hot.

4 ▲ Pour oil into a frying pan to a depth of about 1 in. When hot but not smoking, shallow fry the meatballs for 10–12 minutes, turning them 3–4 times and pressing them flat with a spatula. Remove and drain on paper towels. Serve hot, with the peperonata alongside. Garnish with the basil.

Variation

Instead of ground beef, used half ground pork and half ground veal.

Veal Shanks with Tomatoes and White Wine   *Osso buco*

This famous Milanese dish is rich and hearty. It is traditionally served with risotto alla milanese, but plain boiled rice goes equally well. The lemony gremolata garnish helps to cut the richness of the dish, as does a crisp green salad—serve it after the osso buco and before the dessert, to refresh the palate.

Ingredients

2 tbsp flour
4 pieces of osso buco
2 small onions
2 tbsp olive oil
1 large celery stalk, finely chopped
1 medium carrot, finely chopped
2 garlic cloves, finely chopped
1 can (14 oz) chopped tomatoes
1¼ cups dry white wine
1¼ cups chicken or veal stock
1 strip of thinly pared lemon rind
2 bay leaves, plus extra for
    garnishing (optional)
salt and freshly ground black pepper

For the gremolata

2 tbsp finely chopped fresh
    flat-leaf parsley
finely grated rind of 1 lemon
1 garlic clove, finely chopped
serves 4

1 ▲ Preheat the oven to 325ºF. Season the flour with salt and pepper and spread it out in a shallow bowl. Add the pieces of veal and turn them in the flour until evenly coated. Shake off any excess flour.

2 ▲ Slice one of the onions and separate it into rings. Heat the oil in a large flameproof casserole, then add the veal, with the onion rings, and brown the veal on both sides over medium heat. Remove the veal shanks with tongs and set aside on paper towels to drain.

3 ▲ Chop the remaining onion and add it to the pan with the celery, carrot and garlic. Stir the bottom of the pan to incorporate the pan juices and sediment. Cook gently, stirring frequently, for about 5 minutes, until the vegetables soften slightly.

4 ▲ Add the chopped tomatoes, wine, stock, lemon rind and bay leaves, then season to taste with salt and pepper. Bring to a boil, stirring. Return the veal to the pan and coat with the sauce. Cover and cook in the oven for 2 hours or until the veal feels tender when pierced with a fork.

5 Meanwhile, make the gremolata. In a small bowl, combine the chopped parsley, lemon rind and chopped garlic. Remove the casserole from the oven and lift out and discard the strip of lemon rind and the bay leaves. Taste the sauce for seasoning. Serve the osso buco hot, sprinkled with the gremolata and garnished with extra bay leaves, if desired.

Cook's Tip

Osso buco is available at large supermarkets and good butchers. Choose pieces about ¾ in thick.

Calf's Liver with Balsamic Vinegar

Fegato all'aceto balsamico

This sweet-and-sour liver dish is a speciality of Venice. Serve it very simply, with green beans sprinkled with browned bread crumbs.

Ingredients

1 tbsp flour
½ tsp finely chopped fresh sage
4 thin slices of calf's liver, cut into
  serving pieces
3 tbsp olive oil
2 tbsp butter
2 small red onions, sliced and separated
  into rings
⅔ cup dry white wine
3 tbsp balsamic vinegar
pinch of sugar
salt and freshly ground black pepper
fresh sprigs of sage, to garnish
green beans sprinkled with browned
  bread crumbs, to serve

serves 2

Cook's Tip

Never overcook calf's liver, because it quickly turns tough. Its delicate flesh is at its most tender when it is served slightly underdone and pink—like a rare steak.

1 ▲ Spread out the flour in a shallow bowl. Season it with the sage and plenty of salt and pepper. Turn the liver in the flour until well coated.

2 Heat 2 tbsp of the oil with half of the butter in a wide heavy saucepan or frying pan until foaming. Add the onion rings and cook gently, stirring frequently, for about 5 minutes, until softened but not colored. Remove with a spatula and set aside.

3 ▲ Heat the remaining oil and butter in the pan until foaming, add the liver and cook over medium heat for 2–3 minutes on each side. Transfer to heated dinner plates and keep hot.

4 Add the wine and vinegar to the pan, then stir to mix with the pan juices and any sediment. Add the onions and sugar and heat through, stirring. Spoon the sauce over the liver, garnish with sage sprigs and serve immediately with the green beans.

Veal Cutlets with Lemon

Scaloppine al limone

Popular in Italian restaurants, this dish is very easy to make at home.

Ingredients

4 veal cutlets
2–3 tbsp flour
4 tbsp butter
¼ cup olive oil
¼ cup Italian dry white vermouth or dry
    white wine
3 tbsp lemon juice
salt and freshly ground black pepper
lemon wedges and fresh parsley, to garnish
green beans and peperonata, to serve

serves 4

1 ▲ Put each cutlet between two sheets of plastic wrap and pound until very thin.

2 Cut the pounded cutlets in halves or quarters, and coat in the flour, seasoned with salt and pepper.

3 ▲ Melt the butter with half the oil in a large, heavy frying pan until sizzling. Add as many cutlets as the pan will hold. Fry over medium to high heat for 1–2 minutes on each side, until lightly colored. Remove with a spatula and keep hot. Add the remaining oil and cook the remaining cutlets in the same way.

4 Remove the pan from the heat and add the vermouth and the lemon juice. Stir vigorously to mix with the pan juices, then return to the heat and return all the veal to the pan. Spoon the sauce over the veal. Shake the pan over medium heat until all of the cutlets are coated in the sauce and heated through.

5 Serve immediately, garnished with lemon wedges and parsley. Lightly cooked green beans and peperonata make a delicious accompaniment.

Variation
Use skinless boneless chicken breasts instead of the veal. If they are thick, cut them in half before pounding.

Roast Lamb with Rosemary

Agnello al rosmarino

In Italy, lamb is traditionally served at Easter. This simple roast with potatoes owes its wonderful flavor to the fresh rosemary and garlic. It makes the perfect Sunday lunch at any time of year, served with one or two lightly cooked fresh vegetables, such as broccoli, spinach or baby carrots.

Ingredients

½ leg of lamb, about 3 lb
2 garlic cloves, cut lengthwise into
    thin slivers
7 tbsp olive oil
leaves from 4 sprigs of fresh rosemary,
    finely chopped
about 1 cup lamb or vegetable stock
1½ pounds potatoes, cut into
    1-in cubes
a few fresh sage leaves, chopped
salt and freshly ground black pepper
lightly cooked baby carrots, to serve
serves 4

1 ▲ Preheat the oven to 450°F. Using the point of a sharp knife, make deep incisions in the lamb, especially near the bone, and insert the slivers of garlic.

2 ▲ Put the lamb in a roasting pan and rub it all over with 3 tbsp of the oil. Sprinkle on about half of the chopped rosemary, patting it on firmly, and season with plenty of salt and pepper. Roast for 30 minutes, turning once.

3 ▲ Lower the oven temperature to 375°F. Turn the lamb over again and add ½ cup of the stock.

4 Roast for 1¼–1½ hours longer until the lamb is tender, turning the joint two or three times more and adding the rest of the stock in two or three batches. Baste the lamb each time it is turned.

5 ▲ Meanwhile, put the potatoes in a separate roasting pan and toss with the remaining oil and rosemary and the sage. Roast, on the same shelf as the lamb if possible, for 45 minutes, turning the potatoes several times until they are golden and tender.

6 ▲ Transfer the lamb to a carving board, tent with foil and set aside in a warm place for 10 minutes so that the flesh firms for easier carving. Serve whole or carved into thin slices, surrounded by the potatoes and accompanied by baby carrots.

Cook's Tip

If desired, the cooking juices can be strained and used to make a thin gravy with stock and red wine.

Pork in Sweet-and-sour Sauce   *Scaloppine di maiale in agrodolce*

The combination of sweet and sour flavors is popular in Venetian cooking, especially with meat and liver. This recipe is given extra bite with the addition of crushed mixed peppercorns. Served with shelled fava beans tossed with grilled bacon—it is delectable.

Ingredients
1 whole pork fillet, about 12 oz
1½ tbsp flour
2–3 tbsp olive oil
1 cup dry white wine
2 tbsp white wine vinegar
2 tsp sugar
1 tbsp mixed peppercorns, coarsely
    ground
salt and freshly ground black pepper
fava beans tossed with grilled bacon,
    to serve

serves 2

3 ▲ Heat 1 tbsp of the oil in a wide heavy saucepan or frying pan and add as many slices of pork as the pan will hold. Fry over medium to high heat for 2–3 minutes on each side, until crispy and tender. Remove with a spatula and set aside. Repeat with the remaining pork, adding more oil as necessary.

4 ▲ Mix the wine, wine vinegar and sugar in a bowl. Pour into the pan and stir vigorously over high heat until reduced, scraping the pan to incorporate the sediment. Stir in the peppercorns and return the pork to the pan. Spoon the sauce over the pork until it is evenly coated and heated through.

1 ▲ Cut the pork diagonally into thin slices. Place between two sheets of plastic wrap and pound lightly with a rolling pin to flatten them evenly.

2 ▲ Spread out the flour in a shallow bowl. Season well and coat the meat.

Cook's Tip
Grind the peppercorns in a pepper grinder, or crush them with a mortar and pestle.

Chicken with Tomatoes and Shrimp *Pollo alla marengo*

This Piedmontese dish was created especially for Napoleon after the battle of Marengo.

Versions of it appear in both Italian and French recipe books.

Ingredients

½ cup olive oil
8 chicken thighs on the bone, skinned
1 onion, finely chopped
1 celery stalk, finely chopped
1 garlic clove, crushed
12 oz ripe Italian plum tomatoes, peeled
    and roughly chopped
1 cup dry white wine
½ tsp finely chopped fresh rosemary
1 tbsp butter
8 small triangles of thinly sliced white
    bread, without crusts
20 large shrimp, shelled
salt and freshly ground black pepper
finely chopped flat-leaf parsley, to garnish

serves 4

1 ▲ Heat about 2 tbsp of the oil in a frying pan, add the chicken thighs and sauté over medium heat for about 5 minutes, until they have changed color on all sides. Transfer to a flameproof casserole.

2 ▲ Add the onion and celery to the frying pan and cook gently, stirring frequently, for about 3 minutes, until softened. Add the garlic, tomatoes, wine, rosemary and salt and pepper to taste. Bring to a boil, stirring.

3 Pour the tomato sauce over the chicken. Cover and cook gently for 40 minutes or until the chicken is tender when pierced.

4 ▲ About 10 minutes before serving, add the remaining oil and the butter to the frying pan and heat until hot but not smoking. Add the triangles of bread and shallow fry until crisp and golden on each side. Drain on paper towels.

5 ▲ Add the shrimp to the tomato sauce and heat until the shrimp are cooked. Taste the sauce for seasoning. Dip one of the tips of each fried bread triangle in parsley. Serve the dish hot, garnished with the bread triangles.

Variation

To make the dish look more like its original, authentic version, garnish it with a few large crayfish or shrimp in their shells.

Chicken with Chianti

Pollo al chianti

Together the robust, full-flavored red wine and red pesto give this sauce a rich color and almost spicy flavor, while the grapes add a delicious sweetness. Serve the stew with grilled polenta or warm crusty bread, and accompany with piquant greens, such as arugula or watercress, tossed with a tasty dressing.

Ingredients

3 tbsp olive oil
4 part-boned chicken breasts, skinned
1 medium red onion
2 tbsp red pesto
1¼ cups Chianti
1¼ cups water
4 oz red grapes, halved lengthwise and
    seeded if necessary
salt and freshly ground black pepper
fresh basil leaves, to garnish
arugula salad, to serve

serves 4

1 ▲ Heat 2 tbsp of the oil in a large frying pan, add the chicken breasts and sauté over medium heat for about 5 minutes until they have changed color on all sides. Remove with a slotted spoon and drain on paper towels.

Cook's Tip

Use part-boned chicken breasts, if you can get them, in preference to boneless chicken for this dish, as they have a better flavor. Chicken thighs or drumsticks could also be cooked in this way.

2 Cut the onion in half, through the root. Trim off the root, then slice the onion halves lengthwise to create thin wedges.

3 ▲ Heat the remaining oil in the pan, add the onion wedges and red pesto and cook gently, stirring constantly, for about 3 minutes, until the onion is softened, but not browned.

4 ▲ Add the Chianti and water to the pan and bring to a boil, stirring, then return the chicken to the pan and add salt and pepper to taste.

5 Reduce the heat, then cover the pan and simmer gently for about 20 minutes or until the chicken is tender, stirring occasionally.

6 ▲ Add the grapes to the pan and cook over low to medium heat until heated through, then taste the sauce for seasoning. Serve the chicken hot, garnished with basil and accompanied by the arugula salad.

Variations

Use green pesto instead of red, and substitute a dry white wine such as pinot grigio for the Chianti, then finish with seedless green grapes. A few spoonfuls of mascarpone cheese can be added at the end if desired, to enrich the sauce.

Chicken with Prosciutto and Cheese   *Pollo alla valdostana*

The name Valdostana is derived from Val d'Aosta, home of the Fontina cheese used here.

Ingredients
2 thin slices of prosciutto
2 thin slices of Fontina cheese
4 part-boned chicken breasts
4 sprigs of basil
2 tbsp olive oil
1 tbsp butter
1/2 cup dry white wine
salt and freshly ground black pepper
tender young salad greens, to serve
serves 4

Cook's Tip
There is nothing quite like the buttery texture and nutty flavor of Fontina cheese, and it also has superb melting qualities, but you could use a Swiss or French mountain cheese, such as Gruyère or Emmental. Ask for the cheese to be sliced thinly on the machine slicer, as you will find it difficult to slice it thinly yourself.

1 ▲ Preheat the oven to 400°F. Lightly oil a baking dish. Cut the prosciutto and Fontina slices in half crosswise. Skin the chicken breasts, open out the slit in the center of each one, and fill each cavity with half a ham slice and a basil sprig.

2 ▲ Heat the oil and butter in a wide heavy frying pan until foaming. Cook the chicken breasts over medium heat for 1–2 minutes on each side, until they change color. Transfer to the baking dish. Add the wine to the pan juices, stir until sizzling, then pour over the chicken and season to taste.

3 Top each chicken breast with a slice of Fontina. Bake for 20 minutes or until the chicken is tender. Serve hot, with tender young salad greens.

Deviled Chicken   *Pollo alla diavola*

You can tell this spicy, barbecued chicken dish comes from southern Italy because it has dried red chilies in the marinade. Versions without the chilies are just as good.

Ingredients
1/2 cup olive oil
finely grated rind and juice of
    1 large lemon
2 garlic cloves, finely chopped
2 tsp finely chopped or crumbled dried
    red chilies
12 skinless, boneless chicken thighs,
    each cut into 3 or 4 pieces
salt and freshly ground black pepper
flat-leaf parsley leaves, to garnish
lemon wedges, to serve
serves 4

Cook's Tip
Thread the chicken pieces spiral-fashion on the skewers so they do not fall off during cooking.

1 ▲ Make a marinade by mixing the oil, lemon rind and juice, garlic and chilies in a large, shallow glass or china dish. Add salt and pepper to taste. Whisk well, then add the chicken pieces, turning to coat with the marinade. Cover and marinate in the refrigerator for at least 4 hours or, preferably, overnight.

2 ▲ When ready to cook, prepare the barbecue or preheat the broiler and thread the chicken pieces onto eight oiled metal skewers. Cook on the barbecue or under a hot broiler for 6–8 minutes, turning frequently, until tender. Garnish with parsley leaves and serve hot, with lemon wedges.

Vegetables & Salads

· ·

There is no shortage of fresh and delicious vegetables in Italy, and the dishes are imaginative and varied. Most Italian cooks buy only when the vegetables are in season and at their best, so you will rarely find winter and summer vegetables together in one dish. The list of irresistible salad combinations, however, is endless, often with roasted ingredients stirred into crisp green leaves.

Roasted Plum Tomatoes and Garlic

Pomodori al forno

These are so simple to prepare, yet taste absolutely wonderful. Use a large, shallow

earthenware dish that will allow the tomatoes to sear and char in a hot oven.

Ingredients

8 plum tomatoes, halved
12 garlic cloves
1/4 cup extra virgin olive oil
3 bay leaves
salt and freshly ground black pepper
3 tbsp fresh oregano leaves,
    to garnish

serves 4

Cook's Tip

Use ripe plum tomatoes for this
recipe, as they keep their shape and
do not fall apart when roasted at
such a high temperature. Leave the
stalks on, if possible.

1 ▲ Preheat the oven to 450°F. Select
an ovenproof dish that will hold all
the tomatoes snugly in a single layer.
Place the tomatoes in the dish and
push the whole, unpeeled garlic
cloves between them.

2 ▲ Brush the tomatoes with the oil,
add the bay leaves and sprinkle black
pepper over the top. Bake for about
45 minutes, until the tomatoes have
softened and are sizzling in the pan.
They should be charred around the
edges. Season with salt and a little
more black pepper, if needed.
Garnish with oregano and serve.

Green Beans with Tomatoes

Fagiolini al pomodoro

This is a real summer favorite using the best ripe plum tomatoes and green beans.

Ingredients

2 tbsp olive oil
1 large onion, finely sliced
2 garlic cloves, finely chopped
6 large ripe plum tomatoes, peeled,
   seeded and coarsely chopped
²/₃ cup dry white wine
1 lb green beans, sliced in half
   lengthwise
16 pitted black olives
2 tsp lemon juice
salt and freshly ground black pepper

serves 4

Cook's Tip

Green beans need little preparation
and now that they are grown without
the string, you simply trim the ends.
When choosing make sure that the
beans snap easily—this is a good sign
of freshness.

1 ▲ Heat the oil in a large frying pan.
Add the onion and garlic and cook
for about 5 minutes, until the onion
is softened but not brown.

2 ▲ Add the chopped tomatoes,
white wine, beans, olives and lemon
juice and cook over low heat for
20 more minutes, stirring
occasionally, until the sauce is
thickened and the beans are tender.
Season with salt and pepper to
taste and serve immediately.

Fennel Gratin

Finocchi gratinati

This is one of the best ways to eat fresh fennel. The fennel takes on a delicious, almost creamy, flavor, which contrasts beautifully with the sharp, strong Gruyère.

Ingredients
2 fennel bulbs, about 1½ lb
   total weight
1¼ cups milk
1 tbsp butter, plus extra
   for greasing
1 tbsp flour
scant ½ cup dry white bread crumbs
3 oz Gruyère cheese, grated
salt and freshly ground black pepper
serves 4

Cook's Tip
Instead of the Gruyère, Parmesan, Pecorino or any other strong cheese would work perfectly.

1 ▲ Preheat the oven to 475°F. Discard the stalks and root ends from the fennel. Slice into quarters and place in a large saucepan. Pour in the milk and simmer for 10–15 minutes until tender. Butter a baking dish.

2 Remove the fennel pieces with a slotted spoon, reserving the milk, and arrange the fennel pieces in the dish.

3 ▲ Melt the butter in a small saucepan and add the flour, stir well, then gradually whisk in the reserved milk. Stir the sauce until thickened.

4 Pour the sauce over the fennel pieces, and sprinkle with the bread crumbs and grated Gruyère. Season with salt and black pepper and bake for about 20 minutes, until browned.

Sweet-and-sour Onions

Cipolline in agrodolce

Onions are naturally sweet, and when they are cooked at a high temperature the sweetness intensifies. Serve with roasts and meat dishes or as part of an antipasto.

Ingredients
4 tbsp butter
5 tbsp sugar
½ cup white wine vinegar
2 tbsp balsamic vinegar
1½ lb small pickling onions, peeled
salt and freshly ground black pepper
serves 4

Cook's Tips
This recipe also looks and tastes delicious when made with either yellow or red onions, which are cut into either thin slices or chunks. Cooking times will vary, depending on the size of the onion pieces.

1 ▲ Heat the butter in a large saucepan over low heat. Add the sugar and heat until dissolved, stirring constantly.

2 ▲ Add the vinegars to the pan with the onions and combine well. Season with salt and pepper and cover and cook over medium heat for 20–25 minutes, until the onions are a golden color and soft when pierced with a knife. Serve hot.

Roasted Potatoes with Red Onions

Patate al forno

These mouth-watering potatoes are a fine accompaniment to just about anything. The key is to use small firm potatoes; the smaller they are cut, the quicker they will cook.

Ingredients

1½ lb small firm potatoes
2 tbsp butter
2 tbsp olive oil
2 red onions, cut into chunks
8 garlic cloves, unpeeled
2 tbsp chopped fresh rosemary
salt and freshly ground black pepper
serves 4

Cook's Tip

To ensure that the potatoes are crisp, make sure they are completely dry before cooking. Resist the urge to turn the potatoes too often. Let them brown on one side before turning. Do not salt the potatoes until the end of cooking—salting beforehand encourages them to release their liquid, making them limp.

1 ▲ Preheat the oven to 450°F. Peel and quarter the potatoes, rinse them well and pat thoroughly dry with paper towels. Place the butter and oil in a roasting pan and place in the oven to heat.

2 ▲ When the butter has melted and is foaming, add the potatoes, red onions, garlic and rosemary. Toss well, then spread out in one layer.

3 Place the pan in the oven and roast for about 25 minutes, until the potatoes are golden and tender when tested with a fork. Shake the pan occasionally to redistribute the potatoes. When cooked, season with salt and pepper.

Radicchio and Chicory Gratin

Radicchio e indivia gratinati

Vegetables such as radicchio and chicory take on a different flavor when cooked in this way. The creamy béchamel combines wonderfully with the bitter leaves.

Ingredients

2 heads radicchio, quartered lengthwise
2 heads chicory, quartered lengthwise
½ cup drained sun-dried tomatoes in oil,
   chopped roughly
2 tbsp butter
1 tbsp flour
1 cup milk
pinch grated nutmeg
½ cup grated Emmenthal cheese
salt and freshly ground black pepper
chopped fresh parsley, to garnish
serves 4

1 ▲ Preheat the oven to 350°F. Grease a 5-cup baking dish. Trim the radicchio and chicory and separate the leaves, discarding any that are damaged or wilted. Quarter them lengthwise and arrange in the baking dish. Scatter on the sun-dried tomatoes, and brush the leaves liberally with the oil from the jar. Sprinkle with salt and pepper and cover with foil. Bake for 15 minutes, then remove the foil and bake for another 10 minutes, until the vegetables are softened.

Cook's Tip

In Italy radicchio and chicory are often grilled outdoors on a barbecue. To do this, simply prepare the vegetables as above and brush with olive oil. Place cut-side down on the grill for 7–10 minutes until browned. Turn and grill until the other side is browned, about 5 minutes longer.

2 ▲ Make the sauce. Place the butter in a small saucepan and melt over medium heat. When the butter is foaming, add the flour and cook for 1 minute, stirring. Remove from the heat and gradually add the milk, whisking constantly. Return to the heat and bring to a boil, them simmer for 2–3 minutes to thicken. Season to taste and add the nutmeg.

3 Pour the sauce over the vegetables and sprinkle with the grated cheese. Bake for about 20 minutes, until golden. Serve immediately, garnished with parsley.

Potato and Pumpkin Pudding

Tortino di patate e zucca

Serve this savory pudding with any rich meat dish or simply with a mixed salad.

Ingredients
3 tbsp olive oil
1 garlic clove, sliced
large wedge (1½ lb) pumpkin, cut into
    ¾-in chunks
12 oz potatoes, unpeeled
2 tbsp butter
scant ½ cup ricotta cheese
⅔ cup grated Parmesan cheese
pinch grated nutmeg
4 eggs, separated
salt and freshly ground black pepper
chopped fresh parsley, to garnish
serves 4

1 Preheat the oven to 400°F. Grease an 8-cup, shallow, oval baking dish.

Cook's Tip
You may process the vegetables in a food processor for a few seconds, but be careful not to overprocess, as they will become very gluey.

2 ▲ Heat the oil in a large frying pan, add the garlic and pumpkin and cook, stirring often to prevent sticking, for 15–20 minutes or until the pumpkin is tender. Meanwhile, cook the potatoes in boiling salted water for 20 minutes, until tender. Drain, leave until cool enough to handle, then peel off the skins. Place the potatoes and pumpkin in a large bowl and mash together well with the butter.

3 Mash the ricotta with a fork until smooth and add to the potato and pumpkin mixture, mixing well.

4 ▲ Stir the Parmesan, nutmeg and plenty of seasoning into the ricotta mixture—it should be smooth and creamy.

5 Add the egg yolks one at a time until mixed in thoroughly.

6 Whisk the egg whites with an electric whisk until they form stiff peaks, then fold gently into the mixture. Spoon into the prepared baking dish and bake for 30 minutes, until golden and firm. Serve hot, garnished with parsley.

Fried Spring Greens

Cavolo fritto

This dish can be served as a vegetable side dish, or it can be enjoyed simply on its own,

with some warm crusty bread.

Ingredients
2 tbsp olive oil
2 tbsp butter
4 strips bacon, chopped
1 large onion, thinly sliced
1 cup dry white wine
2 garlic cloves, finely chopped
2 pounds spring greens, shredded
salt and freshly ground black pepper
serves 4

Cook's Tips
This dish would work just as well using shredded red cabbage and red wine. Let simmer for 10 minutes longer, as red cabbage leaves are slightly tougher than the spring greens.

1 In a large frying pan, heat the oil and butter and add the bacon. Fry for 2 minutes, then add the onions and fry for another 3 minutes, until the onion is beginning to soften.

2 Add the wine and simmer vigorously for 2 minutes to reduce.

3 Reduce the heat and add the garlic, spring greens and salt and pepper. Cook over low heat for about 15 minutes, until the greens are tender. (Cover the pan so that the greens retain their color.) Serve hot.

Fennel, Orange and Arugula Salad

Insalata di finocchio

This light and refreshing salad is ideal to serve with spicy or rich foods.

Ingredients
2 oranges
1 fennel bulb
4 oz arugula leaves
⅓ cup black olives

For the dressing
2 tbsp extra virgin olive oil
1 tbsp balsamic vinegar
1 small garlic clove, crushed
salt and freshly ground black pepper
serves 4

1 With a vegetable peeler, cut strips of rind from the oranges, leaving the pith behind, and cut into thin julienne strips. Cook in boiling water for a few minutes. Drain. Peel the oranges, removing all the white pith. Slice them into thin rounds and discard any seeds.

2 Cut the fennel bulb in half lengthwise and slice across the bulb as thinly as possible, preferably in a food processor fitted with a slicing disc or using a mandoline.

3 ▲ Combine the oranges and fennel in a serving bowl and toss with the arugula leaves.

4 ▲ Combine the oil, vinegar, garlic and seasoning and pour over the salad, toss together well and let stand for a few minutes. Sprinkle with the black olives and julienne strips of orange.

Eggplant, Lemon and Caper Salad

Caponata

This cooked vegetable relish is a classic Sicilian dish, which is delicious served as an accompaniment to cold meats, with pasta or simply on its own with some good crusty bread. Make sure the eggplant is well cooked until it is meltingly soft.

Ingredients
1 large eggplant, about 1½ lb
¼ cup olive oil
grated rind and juice of 1 lemon
2 tbsp capers, rinsed
12 pitted green olives
2 tbsp chopped fresh
    flat-leaf parsley
salt and freshly ground black pepper
serves 4

Cook's Tips
This will taste even better when made the day before. Serve at room temperature. It will keep, covered in the refrigerator, for up to 4 days. To enrich this dish to serve it on its own as a main course, add toasted pine nuts and shavings of Parmesan cheese. Serve with crusty bread.

1 ▲ Cut the eggplant into 1-in cubes. Heat the olive oil in a large frying pan and cook the eggplant cubes over medium heat for about 10 minutes, tossing regularly, until golden and softened. You may need to do this in two batches. Drain on paper towels and sprinkle with a little salt.

2 ▲ Place the eggplant cubes in a large serving bowl, toss with the lemon rind and juice, capers, olives and chopped parsley and season well with salt and pepper. Serve at room temperature.

Spinach and Roast Garlic Salad   *Insalata di spinaci con aglio arrosto*

Don't worry about the amount of garlic in this salad. During roasting, the garlic becomes sweet and subtle and loses its pungent taste.

Ingredients

12 garlic cloves, unpeeled
¼ cup extra virgin olive oil
1 lb baby spinach leaves
½ cup pine nuts, lightly toasted
juice of ½ lemon
salt and freshly ground black pepper
serves 4

Cook's Tip

If spinach is to be served raw in a salad, the leaves need to be young and tender. Wash them well, drain and pat dry with paper towels.

1 ▲ Preheat the oven to 375°F. Place the garlic in a small roasting dish, toss in 2 tbsp of the olive oil and bake for about 15 minutes, until the garlic cloves are slightly charred around the edges.

2 ▲ While still warm, pour the garlic into a salad bowl. Add the spinach, pine nuts, lemon juice, remaining olive oil and a little salt. Toss well and add black pepper to taste. Serve immediately, inviting guests to squeeze the softened garlic purée out of the skin to eat.

Sweet-and-sour Artichoke Salad

Carciofi in salsa agrodolce

Agrodolce is a sweet-and-sour sauce that works perfectly in this salad.

Ingredients

6 small artichokes
juice of 1 lemon
2 tbsp olive oil
2 medium onions, roughly chopped
1 cup fresh or frozen fava beans
1½ cups fresh or frozen peas (shelled)
salt and freshly ground black pepper
fresh mint leaves, to garnish

For the salsa agrodolce

½ cup white wine vinegar
1 tbsp superfine sugar
handful fresh mint leaves, roughly torn
serves 4

3 ▲ Add the peas, season with salt and pepper and cook for 5 more minutes, stirring occasionally, until the vegetables are tender. Strain through a sieve and place all the vegetables in a bowl, let cool, then cover and chill.

4 ▲ To make the salsa agrodolce, mix all the ingredients in a small pan. Heat gently for 2–3 minutes, until the sugar has dissolved. Simmer gently for about 5 minutes, stirring occasionally. Let cool. To serve, drizzle the salsa over the vegetables and garnish with mint leaves.

1 ▲ Peel the outer leaves from the artichokes and cut into quarters. Place the artichokes in a bowl of water with the lemon juice.

2 ▲ Heat the oil in a large saucepan and add the onions. Cook until the onions are golden. Add the beans and stir, then drain the artichokes and add to the pan. Pour in about 1¼ cups of water and cook, covered, for 10–15 minutes.

Bell Pepper and Tomato Salad   *Peperoni arrostiti con pomodori*

This is one of those lovely recipes that brings together perfectly the colors, flavors and textures of southern Italian food. Eat this dish at room temperature with a green salad.

Ingredients
3 red bell peppers
6 large plum tomatoes
1/2 tsp dried red chili flakes
1 red onion, finely sliced
3 garlic cloves, finely chopped
grated rind and juice of 1 lemon
3 tbsp chopped fresh flat-
    leaf parsley
2 tbsp extra virgin olive oil
salt and freshly ground black pepper
black and green olives and extra
    chopped flat-leaf parsley,
    to garnish
serves 4

Cook's Tip
Peppers roasted this way will keep for several weeks. After peeling off the skins, place the pepper pieces in a jar with a tight-fitting lid. Pour enough olive oil over them to cover completely. Store in the refrigerator.

1 ▲ Preheat the oven to 425°F. Place the peppers on a baking sheet and roast, turning occasionally, for 10 minutes or until the skins are almost blackened. Add the tomatoes to the baking sheet and bake for 5 more minutes.

2 Place the peppers in a plastic bag, close the top loosely, trapping in the steam, and then set them aside, with the tomatoes, until they are cool enough to handle.

3 ▲ Carefully pull off the skin from the peppers. Remove the seeds, then chop the peppers and tomatoes roughly and place in a mixing bowl.

4 Add the chili flakes, onion, garlic, lemon rind and juice. Sprinkle on the parsley. Mix well, then transfer to a serving dish. Sprinkle with a little salt, drizzle on the olive oil and scatter olives and extra parsley over the top. Serve at room temperature.

Marinated Zucchini   *Zucchini a scapece*

This is a simple vegetable dish that is prepared all over Italy using the best of the season's zucchini. It can be eaten hot or cold.

Ingredients
4 zucchini
1/4 cup extra virgin olive oil
2 tbsp chopped fresh mint, plus whole
    leaves, to garnish
2 tbsp white wine vinegar
salt and freshly ground black pepper
whole-wheat Italian bread and green
    olives, to serve
serves 4

Cook's Tip
Carrots, green beans, and onions can also be prepared in this way.

1 ▲ Cut the zucchini into thin slices. Heat 2 tbsp of the oil in a wide heavy saucepan. Fry the zucchini in batches, for 4–6 minutes, until tender and brown around the edges. Transfer the zucchini to a bowl. Season well.

2 ▲ Heat the remaining oil in the pan, then add the mint and vinegar and let it bubble for a few seconds. Pour the marinade over the zucchini. Marinate for 1 hour, then serve garnished with mint and accompanied by bread and olives.

Stuffed Eggplants

Melanzane alla ligure

This typical Ligurian dish is spiked with paprika and allspice, a legacy from the days when spices from the East came into northern Italy via the port of Genoa.

Ingredients

2 eggplants, about 8 oz each, stalks
　removed
10 oz potatoes, peeled and diced
2 tbsp olive oil
1 small onion, finely chopped
1 garlic clove, finely chopped
good pinch of ground allspice and paprika
1 egg, beaten
$\frac{1}{2}$ cup grated Parmesan cheese
1 tbsp fresh white bread crumbs
salt and freshly ground black pepper
fresh mint sprigs, to garnish
salad greens, to serve

serves 4

1 Bring a large saucepan of lightly salted water to a boil. Add the whole eggplant and cook for 5 minutes, turning frequently. Remove with a slotted spoon and set aside. Add the potatoes to the pan and cook for 20 minutes until soft.

2 ▲ Meanwhile, cut the eggplants in half lengthwise and gently scoop out the flesh with a small sharp knife and a spoon, leaving $\frac{1}{4}$ in of the shell intact. Select a baking dish that will hold the eggplant shells snugly in a single layer. Brush it lightly with oil. Put the shells in the baking dish and chop the eggplant flesh roughly.

Cook's Tip
The eggplants can be filled in advance, then covered with foil and kept in the refrigerator. Add the crumb topping just before baking.

3 ▲ Heat the oil in a frying pan, add the onion and cook gently, stirring frequently, until softened. Add the chopped eggplant flesh and the garlic. Cook, stirring frequently, for 6–8 minutes. Pour into a bowl. Preheat the oven to 375°F.

4 Drain and mash the potatoes. Add the spices and beaten egg to the eggplant mixture. Set aside 1 tbsp of the Parmesan and add the rest to the eggplant mixture, stir in salt and pepper to taste.

5 ▲ Spoon the mixture into the eggplant shells. Mix the bread crumbs with the reserved Parmesan cheese and sprinkle the mixture onto the eggplants. Bake for 40–45 minutes, until the topping is crisp. Garnish with mint and serve with salad greens.

Bell Pepper Gratin

Peperoni gratinati

Serve this simple but delicious dish as an appetizer with a small mixed leaf or arugula

salad and some good crusty bread to mop up the juices from the peppers.

Ingredients

2 red bell peppers
2 tbsp extra virgin olive oil
¼ cup fresh white bread crumbs
1 garlic clove, finely chopped
1 tsp drained bottled capers
8 pitted black olives, roughly chopped
1 tbsp chopped fresh oregano
1 tbsp chopped fresh flat-
    leaf parsley
salt and freshly ground black pepper
fresh herbs, to garnish

serves 4

1 ▲ Preheat the oven to 400°F. Place the peppers under a hot broiler. Turn occasionally until they are blackened and blistered all over. Remove from the heat and place in a plastic bag. Seal and let cool.

2 ▲ When cool, peel the peppers. (Don't skin them under the tap, as the water would wash away some of the delicious smoky flavor.) Halve and remove the seeds, then cut the flesh into large strips.

3 ▲ Use a little of the olive oil to grease a small baking dish. Arrange the pepper strips in the dish.

4 ▲ Scatter the remaining ingredients on top, drizzle with the remaining olive oil and add salt and pepper to taste. Bake for about 20 minutes, until the bread crumbs have browned. Garnish with fresh herbs and serve immediately.

Desserts

An everyday Italian meal usually concludes with fresh fruit. Desserts are reserved for special occasions, and are often bought at the local pasticceria or gelateria. This is not to say that sweet things are unpopular, but they are usually eaten with a cup of espresso coffee at other times of the day.

Tiramisù

Tiramisù

The name of this popular dessert translates as "pick me up," which is said to derive from the fact that it is so good that it literally makes you swoon when you eat it. There are many, many versions, and the recipe can be adapted to suit your own taste—you can vary the amount of mascarpone, eggs, ladyfingers, coffee and liqueur.

Ingredients

3 eggs, separated
2 cups mascarpone cheese, at room
    temperature
1 tbsp vanilla sugar
³/₄ cup cold, very strong, black coffee
¹/₂ cup Kahlúa or other coffee-flavored
    liqueur
18 savoiardi (Italian ladyfingers)
sifted cocoa powder and grated
    bittersweet chocolate, to finish

serves 6–8

3 ▲ Combine the coffee and liqueur in a shallow dish. Dip a ladyfinger in the mixture, turn it quickly so that it becomes saturated but does not disintegrate, and place it on top of the mascarpone in the bowl. Add five more dipped ladyfingers, placing them side by side.

4 ▲ Spoon in about one-third of the remaining mixture and spread it out. Make more layers in the same way, ending with mascarpone. Level the surface, then sift cocoa powder all over. Cover and chill overnight. Before serving, sprinkle with cocoa and grated chocolate.

1 ▲ Put the egg whites in a grease-free bowl and whisk with an electric mixer until stiff and in peaks.

2 ▲ Mix the mascarpone, vanilla sugar and egg yolks in a separate large bowl and whisk with the electric mixer until evenly combined. Fold in the egg whites, then put a few spoonfuls of the mixture in the bottom of a large serving bowl and spread it out evenly.

Stuffed Peaches with Amaretto

Pesche ripiene

Together amaretti cookies and amaretto liqueur have an intense almond flavor, and they make a natural partner for peaches.

Ingredients

4 ripe but firm peaches
2 oz amaretti cookies
2 tbsp butter, softened
2 tbsp confectioners' sugar
1 egg yolk
¼ cup amaretto liqueur
1 cup dry white wine
8 tiny sprigs of basil, to decorate
ice cream or heavy cream, to serve

serves 4

3 ▲ Cream the butter and sugar in a separate bowl until smooth. Stir in the reserved chopped peach flesh, the egg yolk and half the amaretto liqueur with the amaretti crumbs. Lightly butter a baking dish that is just large enough to hold the peach halves in a single layer.

4 ▲ Spoon the stuffing into the peaches, then stand them in the dish. Mix the remaining liqueur with the wine, pour over the peaches and bake for 25 minutes or until the peaches feel tender when tested with a skewer. Decorate with basil and serve immediately, with ice cream or cream.

1 ▲ Preheat the oven to 350°F. Following the natural indentation line on each peach, cut in half down to the central pit, then twist the halves in opposite directions to separate them. Remove the peach pits, then cut out a little of the central flesh to make a larger hole for the stuffing. Chop this flesh finely and set aside.

2 ▲ Put the amaretti cookies in a bowl and crush them finely with the end of a rolling pin.

Zabaglione

Zabaglione

This sumptuous warm dessert is very quick and easy to make, but it does need to be served immediately. For a dinner party, assemble all the ingredients and equipment ahead of time so that all you have to do is quickly combine everything once the main course is over.

Ingredients
4 egg yolks
1/3 cup confectioners' sugar
1/2 cup dry Marsala
savoiardi (Italian ladyfingers), to serve
serves 6

Cook's Tip
When whisking the egg yolks, make sure that the bottom of the bowl does not touch the water or the egg yolks will scramble.

1 ▲ Half fill a pan with water and bring it to the simmering point. Put the egg yolks and sugar in a large heatproof bowl and beat with a hand-held electric mixer until pale and creamy.

2 ▲ Put the bowl over the pan and gradually pour in the Marsala, whisking the mixture until it is very thick and has increased in volume.

3 Remove the bowl from the water and pour the zabaglione into six heatproof, long-stemmed glasses. Serve immediately, with ladyfingers.

Lovers' Knots

Cenci

The literal translation of cenci is "rags and tatters," but they are often referred to by the more endearing term of lovers' knots. They are eaten at carnival time in February.

Ingredients
1 1/4 cups flour
1/2 tsp baking powder
pinch of salt
2 tbsp confectioners' sugar, plus extra for dusting
1 egg, beaten
about 1 1/2 tbsp rum
vegetable oil, for deep-frying
makes 24

Cook's Tip
If you do not have a deep-fat fryer with a built-in thermostat, or a deep-fat thermometer, test the temperature of the oil before deep-frying by dropping in a scrap of the dough trimmings—it should turn crisp and golden in about 30 seconds.

1 ▲ Sift the flour, baking powder and salt into a bowl, then stir in the sugar. Add the egg. Stir with a fork until it is evenly mixed with the flour, then add the rum gradually and continue mixing until the dough draws together. Knead the dough on a lightly floured surface until it is smooth. Divide the dough into quarters.

2 ▲ Roll each piece out to a 6 x 3-in rectangle and trim to make them straight. Cut each rectangle lengthwise into six strips, 1/2 in wide, and tie into a simple knot.

3 Heat the oil in a deep-fat fryer to a temperature of 375°F. Deep-fry the knots in batches for 1–2 minutes, until crisp and golden. Transfer to paper towels with a slotted spoon. Serve warm, dusted with sugar.

Fresh Orange Granita

Granita all'arancia

A granita is like a sorbet, but coarser and quite grainy in texture, hence its name. It makes a refreshing dessert after a rich main course, or a cooling treat on a hot summer's day.

Ingredients

4 large oranges
1 large lemon
³/₄ cup sugar
2 cups water
blanched pared strips of orange and
lemon rind, to decorate
cookies, to serve

serves 6

1 ▲ Thinly pare the rind from the oranges and lemon, taking care to avoid the bitter white pith, and set aside for the decoration. Cut the fruit in half and squeeze the juice into a bowl. Set aside.

2 Heat the sugar and water in a heavy saucepan, stirring over low heat until the sugar dissolves. Bring to a boil, then boil without stirring for about 10 minutes, until a syrup forms.

3 ▲ Remove the syrup from the heat, add the pieces of orange and lemon rind and shake the pan. Cover and let cool.

4 ▲ Strain the sugar syrup into a shallow freezer container and add the fruit juice. Stir well to mix, then freeze, uncovered, for about 4 hours, until slushy.

Cook's Tip

To make the decoration, slice extra orange and lemon rind into thin strips. Blanch for 2 minutes, refresh under cold water and dry before use.

5 ▲ Remove the half-frozen mixture from the freezer and mix with a fork, then return to the freezer and freeze again for 4 more hours or until frozen hard. To serve, pour into a bowl and let soften for about 10 minutes, then break up with a fork again and pile into long-stemmed glasses. Decorate with the strips of orange and lemon rind and serve with cookies.

Apple Cake

Torta di mele

This moist cake is best served warm. It comes from Genoa, home of the whisked sponge.

When whipping the cream, add grated lemon rind—it tastes delicious.

Ingredients

1½ lb Golden Delicious apples
finely grated rind and juice of
    1 large lemon
4 eggs
¾ cup confectioners' sugar
1¼ cups flour
1 tsp baking powder
pinch of salt
8 tbsp butter, melted and cooled, plus
    extra for greasing
1 tbsp vanilla sugar, for sprinkling
very finely pared strips of citrus rind,
    to decorate
whipped cream, to serve

serves 6

1 ▲ Preheat the oven to 350°F. Brush a 9-in springform pan with melted butter and line the base with parchment paper. Quarter, core and peel the apples, then slice thinly. Put the slices in a bowl and pour in the lemon juice.

2 ▲ Put the eggs, sugar and lemon rind in a bowl and whisk with a hand-held electric mixer until the mixture is thick and mousse-like. The whisks should leave a trail.

3 ▲ Sift half the flour, all the baking powder and the salt over the egg mousse, then fold in gently with a large metal spoon. Slowly drizzle in the melted butter from the side of the bowl and fold it in gently with the spoon. Sift in the remaining flour, fold it in gently, then add the apples and fold these in equally gently.

4 ▲ Spoon into the prepared pan and level the surface. Bake for 40 minutes or until a skewer comes out clean. Let settle in the pan for about 10 minutes, then invert on a wire rack. Turn the cake the right way up and sprinkle the vanilla sugar on top. Decorate with the citrus rind. Serve warm, with whipped cream.

Sicilian Ricotta Cake

Cassata siciliana

The word cassata is often used to describe a layered ice cream cake. In Sicily, however, it is a traditional cake made of layers of sponge, ricotta cheese and candied peel, imbibed with alcohol, and it looks and tastes truly delicious.

Ingredients
3 cups ricotta cheese
finely grated rind of 1 orange
2 tbsp vanilla sugar
5 tbsp orange-flavored liqueur
4 oz candied peel
8 trifle sponge cakes
¼ cup freshly squeezed orange juice
extra candied peel, to decorate
serves 8–10

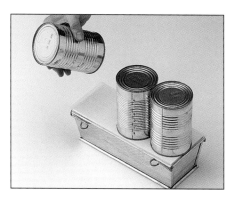

1 ▲ Push the ricotta cheese through a sieve into a bowl, add the orange rind, vanilla sugar and 1 tbsp of the liqueur and beat well to mix. Transfer about one-third of the mixture to another bowl, cover and chill until serving time.

2 ▲ Finely chop the candied peel and beat into the remaining ricotta cheese mixture until evenly mixed. Set aside while you prepare the pan.

3 ▲ Line the base of a 5-cup loaf pan with non-stick baking paper. Cut the trifle sponges in half through their thickness. Arrange four pieces of sponge side by side in the bottom of the loaf pan and sprinkle with 1 tbsp each of liqueur and orange juice.

4 ▲ Put one-third of the ricotta and fruit mixture in the pan and spread it out evenly. Cover with four more pieces of sponge and sprinkle with another 1 tbsp each liqueur and orange juice as before.

5 Repeat the alternate layers of ricotta mixture and sponge until all the ingredients are used, soaking the sponge pieces with liqueur and orange juice each time, and ending with soaked sponge. Cover with a piece of parchment paper.

6 ▲ Cut a piece of cardboard to fit inside the pan, place on top of the parchment paper and weight down evenly. Chill for 24 hours.

7 Remove the weights, cardboard and paper and run a spatula between the sides of the cassata and the pan. Invert a serving plate on top of the cassata, then invert the two so that the cassata is upside down on the plate. Peel off the lining paper.

8 Spread the chilled ricotta mixture over the cassata to cover it completely, then decorate the top with candied peel, cut into fancy shapes. Serve chilled.

Cook's Tip
Don't worry if the cassata has pressed into an uneven shape when turned out. This will be disguised when the cake is covered in the chilled ricotta mixture.

Coffee and Chocolate Bombe

Zuccotto

In Italy the commercial ice cream is so good that no one would dream of making their own ice cream for this dessert. Assembling the zuccotto is impressive enough in itself.

Ingredients
15–18 savoiardi (Italian ladyfingers)
about ¾ cup sweet Marsala
3 oz amaretti cookies
about 2 cups coffee ice
    cream, softened
about 2 cups vanilla ice
    cream, softened
2 oz bittersweet or plain
    chocolate, grated
chocolate curls and sifted cocoa powder
    or confectioners' sugar, to decorate
serves 6–8

1 ▲ Line a 4-cup soufflé dish with a large piece of damp muslin, letting it hang over the top edge. Trim the ladyfingers to fit the basin, if necessary. Pour the Marsala into a shallow dish. Dip a ladyfinger in the Marsala, turning it quickly so that it becomes saturated but does not disintegrate. Stand it against the side of the basin, sugared-side out. Repeat with the remaining sponge fingers to line the basin fully.

2 Fill in the base and any gaps around the side with any trimmings and savoiardi cut to fit. Chill for about 30 minutes.

Cook's Tip
In Italy there are special dome-shaped molds for making this dessert, the name for which comes from the Italian word zucca, meaning pumpkin. The shape will not be quite the same when it is made in a soufflé dish.

3 ▲ Put the amaretti cookies in a large bowl and crush them with a rolling pin. Add the coffee ice cream and any remaining Marsala and beat until mixed. Spoon into the ladyfinger-lined dish.

4 Press the ice cream against the sponge to form an even layer with a hollow. Freeze for 2 hours.

5 Put the vanilla ice cream and grated chocolate in a bowl and beat together until evenly mixed. Spoon into the hollow in the center of the mold. Smooth the top, then cover with the overhanging muslin. Place in the freezer overnight.

6 To serve, run a spatula between the muslin and the basin, then unfold the top of the muslin. Invert a chilled serving plate on top of the zuccotto, then invert the two so that the zuccotto is upside down on the plate. Carefully peel off the muslin. Decorate the zuccotto with the chocolate curls, then sift cocoa powder or confectioners' sugar over. Serve immediately.

Ricotta Pudding

Budino di ricotta

This creamy, rich dessert is very easy to make and, as it can be made up to 24 hours ahead, it is ideal for a dinner party. The combination of ricotta cheese and candied fruits is very popular in Sicily, where this recipe originated.

Ingredients

1 cup ricotta cheese
1/3 cup candied fruits
1/4 cup sweet Marsala
1 cup heavy cream
1/4 cup confectioners' sugar, plus extra
   to serve
finely grated rind of 1 orange
2 cups fresh raspberries
strips of thinly pared orange rind,
   to decorate

serves 4–6

Cook's Tip

Buy candied fruits in large pieces at a good gourmet food store—the chopped candied peel in tubs is too tough to eat raw, and should only be used in baking.

1 ▲ Press the ricotta through a sieve into a bowl. Finely chop the candied fruits and stir into the sieved ricotta with half of the Marsala. Put the cream, sugar and orange rind in another bowl and whip until the cream is standing in soft peaks.

2 ▲ Fold the whipped cream into the ricotta mixture. Spoon into individual glass serving bowls and top with the raspberries. Chill until serving time. Sprinkle with the remaining Marsala and dust the top of each bowl liberally with confectioners' sugar just before serving. Decorate with the orange rind.

Baking

··

The Italian tradition of baking dates back to Roman times, and Italian bakers and pastry chefs today take enormous pride in their art. Baking at home is generally simple—rustic breads, pies and tarts, the occasional cheesecake or batch of cookies. Elaborate confections are usually left to the professionals.

Focaccia with Olives

Focaccia con olive

For this topping, pieces of pitted green olives are pressed onto the dough before baking.

Ingredients
1 recipe Basic Pizza Dough, risen once
3 tbsp olive oil
10–12 large green olives, pitted and cut in
  half lengthwise
coarse sea salt
serves 6–8 as a side dish

1 After punching the dough down,
knead it for 3–4 minutes. Brush a large
shallow baking pan with 1 tbsp of the
oil. Place the dough in the pan, and use
your fingers to press it into an even
layer 1 inch thick. Cover the dough
with a cloth, and leave to rise in a
warm place for 30 minutes. Preheat
the oven to 400°F for 30 minutes
during this time.

2 ▲ Just before baking, use your
fingers to press rows of light
indentations into the surface of the
focaccia. Brush with the remaining oil.

3 ▲ Dot evenly with the olive pieces,
and sprinkle with a little coarse salt.
Bake for about 25 minutes, or until
just golden. Cut into squares or
wedges and serve as an
accompaniment to a meal, or alone,
warm or at room temperature.

Focaccia with Rosemary

Focaccia con rosmarino

One of the most popular breads. If possible, use fresh rosemary for this recipe.

Ingredients
1 recipe Basic Pizza Dough, risen once
3 tbsp olive oil
2 medium sprigs fresh rosemary, coarse
  stalks removed
coarse sea salt
serves 6–8 as a side dish

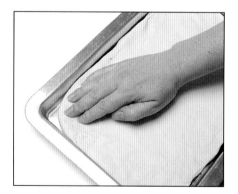

1 ▲ After punching the dough down,
knead it for 3–4 minutes. Brush a large
shallow baking pan with 1 tbsp of the
oil. Place the dough in the pan, and use
your fingers to press it into an even
layer 1 inch thick.

2 ▲ Scatter with the rosemary leaves.
Cover the dough with a cloth, and
leave to rise in a warm place for 30
minutes. Preheat the oven to 400°F for
30 minutes during this time.

3 ▲ Just before baking, use your
fingers to press rows of light
indentations into the surface of the
focaccia. Brush with the remaining oil,
and sprinkle lightly with coarse salt.
Bake for about 25 minutes, or until
just golden. Cut into squares or
wedges and serve as an
accompaniment to a meal, or alone,
warm or at room temperature.

Raisin and Walnut Bread

Pane di uva con noci

This bread is delicious with soup for a first course, or with salami, cheese and salad for lunch. It tastes good with jam and toasts extremely well when it is a day or two old.

Ingredients
2¾ cups flour
½ tsp salt
1 tbsp butter
1½ tsp active dry yeast
scant 1 cup golden raisins
½ cup walnuts, roughly chopped
melted butter, for brushing
makes 1 loaf

1 ▲ Sift the flour and salt into a bowl, cut in the butter with a knife, then stir in the yeast.

2 ▲ Gradually add ¾ cup tepid water to the flour mixture, stirring with a spoon at first, then gathering the dough together with your hands.

3 Turn the dough out onto a floured surface and knead for about 10 minutes, until smooth and elastic.

Cook's Tip
Active dried yeast is sold in envelopes at most supermarkets. It is a real boon for the busy cook because it eliminates the need to let the dough rise before shaping.

4 ▲ Knead the raisins and walnuts into the dough until they are evenly distributed. Shape into a rough oval, place on a lightly oiled baking sheet and cover with oiled plastic wrap. Let rise in a warm place for 1–2 hours, until doubled in bulk. Preheat the oven to 425°F.

5 Uncover the loaf and bake for 10 minutes, then reduce the oven temperature to 375°F and bake for 20–25 more minutes.

6 ▲ Transfer to a wire rack, brush with melted butter and cover with a dish towel. Cool before slicing.

Chocolate Bread

Pane al cioccolato

In Italy it is the custom to serve this dessert bread as a snack with mascarpone or Gorgonzola cheese and a glass of red wine. Although this combination may sound unusual, it is really delicious. Chocolate bread also tastes good spread with butter, and is excellent toasted the next day for breakfast and served with butter and jam.

Ingredients

4 cups flour
½ tsp salt
2 tbsp butter
2 tbsp confectioners' sugar
2 tsp active dry yeast
2 tbsp cocoa powder
½ cup chocolate chips
melted butter, for brushing
makes 2 loaves

1 ▲ Sift the flour and salt into a bowl, cut in the butter with a knife, then stir in the sugar, yeast and cocoa powder.

2 Gradually add 1¼ cups of tepid water to the flour mixture, stirring with a spoon at first, then gathering the dough together with your hands.

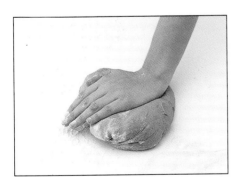

3 ▲ Turn the dough out onto a floured surface and knead for about 10 minutes, until smooth and elastic.

4 ▲ Cut the dough in half and knead half the chocolate chips into each piece of dough until they are evenly distributed. Shape into rounds, place on lightly oiled baking sheets and cover with oiled plastic wrap. Let rise in a warm place for 1–2 hours, until the dough has doubled in bulk.

5 Preheat the oven to 425°F. Uncover the loaves and bake for 10 minutes, then reduce the oven temperature to 375°F and bake for 15–20 more minutes.

6 ▲ Place the loaves on a wire rack and brush liberally with butter. Cover with a dish towel and let cool.

Ricotta Cheesecake

Crostata di ricotta

Low-fat ricotta cheese is excellent for cheesecake fillings because it has a good, firm

texture. Here it is enriched with eggs and cream and enlivened with tangy orange and

lemon rind to make a Sicilian-style dessert.

Ingredients

2 cups low-fat ricotta cheese
½ cup heavy cream
2 eggs
1 egg yolk
⅓ cup confectioners' sugar
finely grated rind of 1 orange
finely grated rind of 1 lemon

For the pastry

1½ cups flour
3 tbsp sugar
pinch of salt
8 tbsp chilled butter, diced
1 egg yolk

serves 8

1 ▲ Make the pastry. Sift the flour, sugar and salt onto a cold work surface. Make a well in the center and put in the diced butter and egg yolk. Gradually work the flour into the diced butter and egg yolk, using your fingertips.

Variations

Add ⅓–⅔ cup finely chopped candied peel to the filling in step 3 (or use ⅓ cup chocolate chips). For a really rich dessert, you can add both candied peel and some grated plain chocolate.

2 ▲ Gather the dough together, reserve about a quarter for the lattice, then press the rest into a 9-in fluted tart pan with a removable base. Chill the pastry shell for 30 minutes.

3 ▲ Meanwhile, preheat the oven to 375°F and make the filling. Put all the ricotta, cream, eggs, egg yolk, sugar and orange and lemon rinds in a large bowl and beat until evenly mixed.

4 ▲ Prick the bottom of the pastry shell, then line with foil and fill with baking beans. Bake blind for 15 minutes, then transfer to a wire rack, remove the foil and beans and allow the tart shell to cool in the pan.

5 ▲ Spoon the cheese and cream filling into the pastry case and level the surface. Roll out the reserved dough and cut into strips. Arrange the strips on the top of the filling in a lattice pattern, sticking them in place with water.

6 Bake for 30–35 minutes, until golden and set. Transfer to a wire rack and let cool, then carefully remove the side of the pan, leaving the cheesecake on the pan base.

Pine Nut Tart

Pinolata

Strange though it may seem, this traditional tart is an Italian version of the rustic

Bakewell tart from Derbyshire in England.

Ingredients

8 tbsp butter, softened
generous ¹/₂ cup confectioners' sugar
1 egg
2 egg yolks
1¹/₄ cups ground almonds
1 cup pine nuts
¹/₄ cup seedless raspberry jam
confectioners' sugar, for dusting
whipped cream, to serve (optional)

For the pastry

1¹/₂ cups flour
¹/₃ cup confectioners' sugar
¹/₄ tsp baking powder
pinch of salt
8 tbsp chilled butter, diced
1 egg yolk

serves 8

1 ▲ Make the pastry. Sift the flour, sugar, baking powder and salt onto a cold work surface. Make a well in the center and put in the diced butter and egg yolk. Gradually work the flour into the butter and egg yolk, using your fingertips.

2 ▲ Gather the dough together, then press it into a 9-in fluted tart pan with a removable base. Chill for 30 minutes.

3 ▲ Meanwhile, make the filling. Cream the butter and sugar with an electric mixer until light and fluffy, then beat in the egg and egg yolks a little at a time, alternating them with the ground almonds. Beat in the pine nuts.

Cook's Tip

This pastry is too sticky to roll out, so simply mold it into the bottom and sides of the pan with your fingertips.

4 ▲ Preheat the oven to 325°F. Spread the jam over the pastry shell, then spoon in the filling. Bake for 30–35 minutes or until a skewer inserted in the center of the tart comes out clean.

5 Transfer to a wire rack and let cool, then carefully remove the side of the pan, leaving the tart on the pan base. Dust with confectioners' sugar and serve with whipped cream, if desired.

Baked Sweet Ravioli

Ravioli dolci al forno

These delicious sweet ravioli are made with a rich pastry flavored with lemon and filled with the traditional ingredients used in Sicilian cassata.

Ingredients

2 cups flour
⅓ cup superfine sugar
8 tbsp butter
1 egg
1 tsp finely grated lemon rind
confectioners' sugar and grated
    chocolate, for sprinkling

For the filling

¾ cup ricotta cheese
¼ cup confectioners' sugar
¾ tsp vanilla extract
1 medium egg yolk
1 tbsp mixed candied fruits or mixed
    citrus peel
1 oz dark chocolate, finely chopped or
    grated
1 small egg, beaten

serves 4

1 Put the flour and sugar into a food processor and, working on full speed, add the butter in pieces until fully worked into the mixture. With the food processor still running, add the egg and lemon rind. The mixture should form a dough that just holds together. Scrape the dough onto a sheet of plastic wrap, cover with another sheet, flatten and chill until needed.

2 ▲ To make the filling, push the ricotta through a sieve into a bowl. Stir in the sugar, vanilla extract, egg yolk, peel and chocolate until combined.

3 ▲ Remove the pastry from the refrigerator and let it come to room temperature. Divide the pastry in half and roll each half between sheets of plastic wrap to make strips, measuring 6 x 22 in. Preheat the oven to 350°F.

4 Arrange heaping spoonfuls of the filling in two rows along one of the pastry strips, ensuring there is at least 1 in clear space around each spoonful. Brush the pastry between the dollops of filling with beaten egg. Place the second strip of pastry on top and press down between each mound of filling to seal.

5 Using a 2½-in plain cookie cutter, cut around each mound of filling to make circular ravioli. Lift each one and, with your fingertips, seal the edges. Place the ravioli on a greased baking sheet and bake for 15 minutes, until golden brown. Serve warm sprinkled with confectioners' sugar and grated chocolate.

Spicy Fruit Cake from Siena

Panforte di Siena

This is a delicious flat cake with a wonderful spicy flavor. Panforte is very rich, so should be cut into small wedges—offer a glass of sparkling wine to go with it.

Ingredients

butter for greasing
1 cup hazelnuts, roughly chopped
½ cup whole almonds, roughly chopped
1⅓ cups mixed candied
    fruits, diced
¼ tsp ground coriander
¾ tsp ground cinnamon
¼ tsp ground cloves
¼ tsp grated nutmeg
½ cup flour
½ cup honey
generous 1 cup sugar
confectioners' sugar, for dusting

serves 12–14

1 Preheat the oven to 350°F. Grease an 8-in round cake pan with the butter. Line the base of the pan with parchment paper.

2 ▲ Spread the nuts on a baking tray and place in the oven for about 10 minutes, until lightly toasted. Remove and set aside. Lower the oven temperature to 300°F.

3 In a large mixing bowl combine the candied fruits, all the spices and the flour and stir together with a wooden spoon. Add the nuts and stir in thoroughly.

Cook's Tip

This will store in an airtight container for up to 2 weeks.

4 ▲ In a small heavy saucepan, stir together the honey and sugar and bring to a boil. Cook the mixture until it reaches 280°F on a sugar thermometer or when a small bit forms a hard ball when pressed between fingertips in ice water. Take care when doing this and use a spoon to remove a little mixture out of the pan for testing.

5 ▲ At this stage, immediately pour the sugar syrup into the dry ingredients and stir in well until evenly coated. Pour into the prepared pan. Dip a spoon into water and use the back of the spoon to press the mixture into the pan. Bake for 1 hour.

6 When ready, it will still feel quite soft but will harden as it cools. Cool completely in the pan and then turn out onto a serving plate. Dust with confectioners' sugar before serving.

Hazelnut Bites

Nocciolini

Serve these sweet little nut cookies as petits fours with after-dinner coffee.

Ingredients

8 tbsp butter, softened
³/₄ cup confectioners' sugar, sifted
1 cup flour
³/₄ cup ground hazelnuts
1 egg yolk
blanched whole hazelnuts, to decorate
confectioners' sugar, to finish
makes about 26

1 ▲ Preheat the oven to 350°F. Line 3–4 baking sheets with parchment paper. Cream the butter and sugar with an electric mixer until light and fluffy.

2 ▲ Beat in the flour, ground hazelnuts and egg yolk until evenly mixed.

Cook's Tip

Don't worry that the cookies are still soft at the end of the baking time— they will harden as they cool.

3 ▲ Take a teaspoonful of the mixture at a time and shape it into a round with your fingers. Place the rounds well apart on the baking paper and press a whole hazelnut into the center of each one.

4 ▲ Bake the cookies, one tray at a time, for about 10 minutes or until golden brown, then transfer to a wire rack and sift over confectioners' sugar over them to cover. Let cool.

Ladies' Kisses

Baci di dama

These old-fashioned Piedmontese cookies make pretty petits fours.

Ingredients
10 tbsp butter, softened
½ cup confectioners' sugar
1 egg yolk
½ tsp almond extract
1 cup ground almonds
1½ cups flour
2 oz chocolate
makes 20

1 Cream the butter and sugar with an electric mixer until light and fluffy, then beat in the egg yolk, almond extract, ground almonds and flour until evenly mixed. Chill until firm, about 2 hours.

2 Preheat the oven to 325°F. Line three or four baking sheets with parchment paper.

3 ▲ Break off small pieces of dough and roll into balls with your hands, making 40 altogether. Place the balls on the baking sheets, spacing them out, as they will spread in the oven.

Cook's Tip
These cookies look extra dainty served in frilly petit four cases.

4 Bake the cookies for 20 minutes or until golden. Remove the baking sheets from the oven, lift off the paper with the cookies on, then place on wire racks. Let the cookies cool on the paper. Repeat with the remaining mixture.

5 ▲ When the cookies are cold, lift them off the paper. Melt the chocolate in a bowl over a pan of hot water. Sandwich the cookies in pairs, with the melted chocolate. Let cool and set before serving.

Tea Cookies

Pastine da the

These cookies are very quick and easy to make. If you don't want to pipe the mixture,

simply spoon it onto the baking paper and press it down with a fork.

Ingredients
10 tbsp butter, softened
¾ cup confectioners' sugar, sifted
1 egg, beaten
a few drops of almond extract
2 cups flour
2–3 large pieces of candied peel
makes 20

Variation
Use 10 candied cherries instead of the candied peel. Cut them in half and press one half, cut-side down, into the center of each cookie.

1 Preheat the oven to 450°F. Line two baking sheets with non-stick baking paper.

2 Cream the butter and sugar with an electric mixer until light and fluffy, then beat in the egg, almond extract and flour until evenly mixed.

3 ▲ Spoon the mixture into a piping bag fitted with a star nozzle and pipe 10 rosette shapes on each of the baking sheets.

4 ▲ Cut the candied peel into small diamond shapes and press one diamond into the center of each cookie, to decorate. Bake for 5 minutes or until golden. Transfer the cookies on the baking paper to a wire rack and let cool. Lift the cookies off the paper when cool.

Index

Index

Index

Acknowledgements

Photographs by William Lingwood
except those on pages 6–9, which
were supplied by John Heseltine.